THE HEALING POWER — OF — SOUND — FOR THE — BLACK COMMUNITY

TERENCE "DOC T" ELLIOTT

I Am Healing in Music books may be purchased for educational, business, or sales promotional use. For information, please email iamhealinginmusic@gmail.com.

First edition

Library of Congress Control Number: 2025922870
Elliott, Terence "Doc T". The Healing Power of Sound for the Black Community / Terence "Doc T" Elliott. - 1.) HEA057000 HEALTH & FITNESS / African American & Black 2.) MUS015000 MUSIC / Ethnomusicology 3.) OCC011010 BODY, MIND & SPIRIT / Healing / Energy (Chakras, Qigong, Reiki)

ISBN 979-8-9936160-1-8 (hardcover)
ISBN 979-8-9936160-0-1 (paperback)
ISBN 979-8-9936160-2-5 (eBook)

Editing by Dr. Terence Elliott
Cover/Interior Design by Samia Asif
Publishing Services by Revision Publishing LLC

DEDICATION
AND ACKNOWLEDGEMENT

The Healing Power of Sound for the Black Community is my effort to compile information on the significance of sound as a therapy for healing. I have been fortunate to learn and work with some giants in the field. Several of them are my teachers, including Baba Mosheh Milon, a master drummer who reminds me that the djembe drum is a healing instrument. Rekhit Kajara, founder of Ra Sekhi Arts, is a Kemetic Reiki healer whom I had the opportunity to learn from and attend her retreat. Baba Fred Johnson, an Afri-Sufic sound healer and jazz vocalist, has taken me under his tutelage, providing me with healing mantras and the knowledge necessary to become a conscious sound healer.

It has been my honor and privilege to work in a community of gifted and committed musicians and sound healers. Fatimah Hanif has been a godsend. Our partnership over the last few years as sound healers has helped me grow and develop, thanks, sis! A personal thanks to the Brothas of the Drum, Michael Spencer and T-Roy Marshall for their continuous friendship and work as drum healers. And a big shout-out to my brother, friend, and educator, Dr. Mtafiti Imara, for encouragement, inspiration, knowledge on resonance, and life.

I am most proud and thankful for a loving family. My wife, Amanda, has been by my side for over forty-five years. We have been able to work together as musicians and sound healers effortlessly. My daughters, Nyeri and Imani, keep me grounded and focused on what matters: my grandchildren, Amaya, Will IV, Malia, and NyLeah, who are my absolute blessing.

Becoming a Sound Therapist has been a life-rewarding journey that has guided me to heal myself, my family, my community, and the world around me. Peace and blessings to my brothers of A²MEND, who have taught me the importance of laughter as a healing mechanism. Minister Imhotep and the Wo'se Community, who remind me of the Soul Power in African Spirituality. Rondy "Chocolate Buddha" Isaac for guiding me to the principles of Yoga and including me as a part of the Barbershop Yoga for Black men, and the Umoja Community for keeping me connected to the work of healing the community.

I dedicate this book to the Creator and the Ancestors, my loving parents, Henry and Lydia Elliott, and all those who have been instrumental in my pilgrimage. Asé

DISCLAIMER

The information, practices, and techniques presented in *The Healing Power of Sound for the Black Community* are intended for educational and cultural enrichment purposes only. This book explores sound healing from historical, cultural, spiritual, and experiential perspectives, particularly as they relate to the traditions and lived experiences of myself and people of African descent.

Sound healing is an alternative holistic practice. Always consult a qualified healthcare provider for advice on any medical condition or before starting a new wellness, therapeutic, or exercise program.

While every effort has been made to present accurate, culturally respectful, and empowering information, the author and publisher disclaim any liability for injury, loss, or damage incurred directly or indirectly because of the use or application of the content in this book.

Readers are encouraged to adapt any practices shared here in ways that are safe, appropriate, and aligned with their own health needs, spiritual beliefs, and community traditions.

TABLE OF CONTENTS

STATEMENT

My birth name is Terence Todd Elliott, but I use Doc T Elliott as my professional name in the field of sound therapy. I have a doctorate in education and over 42 years of experience as an educational leader. My background is characterized by a commitment to learning and self-development, enabling me to be the best I can be. I stand for love by sharing knowledge and modeling my healing for others. My values reflect my upbringing, my family, community, and a connectedness to my African culture and ancestors.

My earliest memory of being touched by the creative spirit was when I was nine or ten years old; my parents bought me a mini keyboard that had letters and numbers on the keys. This made it easy to read music that also included the numbers. I began learning how to play familiar songs and creating my own songs through this process. The piano and music in general have always seemed to call me, and I have been drawn to it as long as I can remember. Even though neither of my parents nor my brother pursued music or showed musical inclinations.

Music has been my voice, even when I did not like to talk much. From elementary school to high school, I was more of an introvert, but I was still somewhat popular. I was never particularly interested in studying music or playing like someone else early on. I enjoyed being creative and composing songs as a means of inner expression. One of my deepest wounds was my father having dementia/Alzheimer's disease, and me not being able to help him overcome it. That is when, in 2007, I first began learning how Music Therapy can help with this disease, and more importantly, I came across the concept of Sound Healing and the progress it was having on dementia patients. My arrival at Sound Healing was too late to have a significant effect on my father. However, it has changed the direction of my life. It made my purpose with music clearer. I have been a performing musician and a music educator for most of my life. Now, my true calling/purpose is to be a Sound Therapist.

On the path toward learning and becoming a Sound Healer, I was told and realized that first I had to deal with my issues and health challenges before I could help others, with the significant problems I have with my mood swings, anxieties, and, mainly, my anger outbursts. I spent and still spend many hours controlling my angry responses to things out of my control. Meditating and toning through humming is a powerful practice for calming the mind and regaining control.

As a certified Sound Therapist, I have introduced the Black community to the benefits of Sound Healing. I conduct workshops, talks, and discussions on the physical and mental health benefits of using music and sound frequencies correctly, and provide Sound Treatments, Sound Baths, and Live-Music Healing Sessions. This book shares my findings and guiding practices for healing myself, my children (and grandchildren), my family, the community, and the world.

IN THE BEGINNING, THERE WAS SOUND

Before words were spoken, there was breath.
Before there was the sound of creation, there was silence.
Before language existed, there was sound, humming the universe into being.

Our Spirit breath is sound.
It is the rhythm of our existence.
It is in our bones, in our blood,
and in the space between our heartbeats.

Listen,
For your mother's hum in the kitchen.
The church choir on Sunday morning.
The crowd protests, chanting in the streets.
The drum that is calling you to remember.
The ancestors who are breathing through your spirit.

Sound is not just music.
It is our medicine.
The vibration mends what was broken,
and lifts our heavy burden.
Calling the scattered pieces back into one's whole self.

Let us not remain silent.
For we are the thunder and the rain.
The moan that carried us through the night.
The shout that split the sky open.
And the happiness that refuses to die.

So let the sound begin.
Let it rise from our belly to our mouth,
from our chest to our hands.
Centered in our feet to the floor that carries the beat.
Let us shake the walls.
Let us bless the air.
Let us reach the ears of those yet unborn.

Because we are here.
Alive and present.
With the echo of every voice that refused to be silenced.
As the song that never ends.

In the beginning, there was sound.
So, let the sound begin.

SOUND IS OUR MEDICINE

This book is written for Black people to heal.

We are living in dark times, marked by hatred and evil, as well as competition and greed. Society seeks material wealth, not love for self and one another. As a melanated people, we are not simply a branch on the human family tree. We are the root, the soil, the original water from which all streams have flowed. The hue that denotes the color of our skin is the same deep richness of the earth that birthed us, as a mark of origin, not of difference. In African cosmology, Blackness is the fertile soil, the dark and infinite space from which all creation emerges, the beginning of all humanity.

Why "Black" is the Preferred Term

The term *Black* is widely embraced because it affirms cultural pride, unity, and a shared history across the African diaspora. Unlike "African American," which primarily refers to U.S. identity, *Black* is more inclusive of global African heritage and is now recognized as a term of dignity, empowerment, and respect when capitalized.

The Origin of Humanity

Modern science, as discovered through fossil evidence and genetic mapping, has confirmed what our stories have conveyed for millennia:

humanity originated in Africa, also known as Alkebulan. Our earliest known ancestors, *Homo sapiens*, walked the lush plains of East Africa nearly 300,000 years ago, carrying with them not only the biological blueprint for all humanity, but also the cultural DNA of song, dance, and spiritual expression.

From the Mitochondrial Eve whose genetic signature flows through every living human, to the migration of our foremothers and forefathers across deserts, savannahs, and seas, African people have been the first storytellers, healers, and musicians. Sound, the human voice, and the drum were our first medicines.

The Sacred Pigment

Melanin is a universal substance primarily recognized as a skin pigment, and it is the central molecule that organizes living systems. Melanin's properties are made up of neurotransmitters that can convert light energy into sound energy and vice versa. Melanin acts like an electrical semiconductor and may even be a superconductor at room temperature. It can bind and release other important molecules and make copies of itself. Because melanin can convert energy from light to sound and back to light, the melanin model provides a strong scientific basis for utilizing light, color, sound, biofeedback, acupuncture, visualization, and other non-drug and non-surgical methods to heal and treat illnesses. The investigation into melanin as a conduit for healing has only commenced. This study shows that Africans were light-years ahead in their efforts to heal.

Melanin, the sacred pigment of our skin, is nature's perfect gift, a biological coloring that protects, absorbs, and transforms sunlight into life-giving energy. It connects us to the rich soils of the Nile Valley, to the volcanic clay of the Rift Valley, to the deep loam of the Congo Basin. In spiritual traditions, we are said to be molded from the very dust of the earth, animated by divine breath.

To be Black is to be of the earth. Our bodies carry the same minerals, waters, and cosmic particles that have cycled through this planet for billions of years. When we hum, sing, or drum, the vibrations we create are not just sounds; they are resonances with the living planet, reminders that we and the Earth are one.

The First Music

Sound has always been our bridge between the seen and the unseen. In Kemet (ancient Egypt), chants were used to align with the Neter, the divine forces of creation. In West Africa, griots preserved the memory of entire communities through the poetry of song. Across the continent, sound was not entertainment; it was life, medicine, prayer, and power.

It was in Africa that humanity discovered that music could heal the body, awaken the spirit, and unite the community in strength. This ancient truth still lives in us. Whether through the sacred hum of "OM" or the vibrational pulse of the talking drum, our sound carries memory, resilience, and transformation.

A Journey Back

This is my journey back to the root, not as a return to the past, but as a reawakening to the source within us. Sound is our inheritance, and it is our medicine. In healing ourselves, we heal our community. In healing our community, we heal the world.

As you step into these chapters, may you hear the echo of the first drum. May you feel the vibration of the earth beneath your feet. May you remember that the sound you make with your voice, your hands, your heart is connected to the very first sound the universe ever made, and Black made that sound.

When we are in pain, we moan.
When we need therapy, we wail.
When we are in our feelings, we sing.

We, the Black community, have always known how to harness our sound, to survive, to mourn, to fight, and to heal. But it seems like somewhere along the way, we began to forget. As the world got louder, we got quieter. Then our sounds were labeled as disruptive. Our voices are now policed, our music commodified, and our vibrations fractured. This manuscript is a remembrance of what we already knew that sound is not just entertainment. Sound is our medicine. It is our spirit. Our energy vibration. It is the frequencies that communicate with the ancestors. It is knowing how to align our nervous systems, speak to our grief, and restore balance to our bodies and communities that have been targeted by trauma.

I wrote this book for my children and their children, for current and aspiring sound healers, yoga instructors, meditation instructors, holistic wellness practitioners, and those who want to root their practice in African and Black diasporic traditions. This also includes Black professionals and athletes who must manage high pressure and chronic stress, for anyone carrying pain in their bodies and music in their spirit, and for those who are ready to reclaim their right to resonate. Throughout these chapters, you will encounter:
- Sacred sound practices from ancient African traditions
- The science of sound and how it heals our trauma
- Rituals, reflections, and community healing tools
- And, most importantly, the essence that our voice is sacred, even if it trembles.

These pages are not here to entertain you. They are here to help you vibrate differently. To remind us of who we are through sound. May this book serve as a reflection of our ancestral wisdom. Let it vibrate through your breath, your spirit, and your home. Let it awaken the songs of the struggle for our people that cannot be silenced. And may these words guide you back to the sound that has always lived within us.

Peace and blessings,

Doc T Elliott

CHAPTER ONE

SOUND TO HEAL BLACK PEOPLE

Sound is a form of vibration, characterized by frequency and energy. For the Black community, sound connects us to our memory, resistance, celebration, grief, liberation, and above all, healing. From ancestral string instruments in Kemet to drumming in West Africa, from the spirituals sung in the cotton fields of the American South to the jazz clubs of Harlem and the hip-hop cyphers of the Bronx, sound has always been our tool of transformation. Sound is our medicine. And in a world where Black bodies are routinely under siege by systemic oppression, trauma, and cultural erasure, healing through sound is not just beneficial; it is necessary.

Sound is a vibrational frequency of energy; it serves as a practice for healing. For Black people in the African continent and across the diaspora, sound has been central to our survival, resistance, and renewal. From the coded spirituals sung under the weight of enslavement to the bass-heavy hip-hop beats that pulse through city blocks, sound has carried not only rhythm, but identity, power, and healing.

An Ancient Relationship with Sound and Breath

We are now learning that the sound of our breath is a sacred thing. The Latin word for spirit, *spiritus* means breath. We must practice breathing exercises and listen to how we inhale and exhale our breath. In pre-colonial

African societies, sound was not just for entertainment; it was a means of communication with the divine. Sound is our connection to both the physical and spiritual aspects of ourselves and others. Chants, melodies, and call-and-response were rituals that aligned the mind, body, and spirit with community. Not just the community of humans, but with nature and all of life.

When our language was prohibited, we hummed or moaned in its place. Because Africans were stolen from various tribal groups, they sailed on ships shackled to others who did not speak their languages or dialects. To communicate, songs were hummed, and their similarity was noticeable due to the shared melodies and rhythms found throughout Africa. For spiritual worship, sound became a sanctuary, a place where harmonies lifted weary souls and reconnected people with God and with one another. Even in pain and trauma, Black people have made sound a tool for transcendence. Sounds of healing can be traced from all around us.

The Healing Power of Everyday Sounds: The Vacuum Cleaner

In the rhythm of daily life, even ordinary household tools can carry healing vibrations. As a young child, I remember my mother vacuuming early Saturday mornings. That sound was so pleasing and comforting; it would put me into a deep sleep. Researching the classic 1960s Hoover upright vacuum cleaner that my mother used. I discovered that its motor produced a steady hum in the range of 100–150 Hz, layered with harmonics that created a rich, droning soundscape. When pressed against the carpet, the brush and suction added textured overtones, forming a constant wave of noise that enveloped the ear.

For many children (like me), this sound acted as a soothing tone. Psychologists suggest that the low-frequency hum resembles the womb environment, where the developing child is surrounded by the steady pulse of blood flow and the resonance of internal organs. This vacuum "drone" also functions like modern white noise machines, masking unpredictable disruptions and replacing them with a steady, uniform vibration. Beyond science, there is also the comfort of associative memory for children; the sound often meant safety, familiarity, and the presence of a parent caring for the home.

Thus, what some might dismiss as mere household noise can, in truth, function as a healing frequency, a reminder that the sonic world around us is full of unexpected pathways to comfort, balance, and calm. It was undoubtedly one of the earliest sounds that I recall as a soothing tone to help me fall asleep and feel at peace.

The Legacy of Sound in Black Life

Throughout history, Black people have turned to sound when words were not enough. In the Middle Passage, moans and hums traveled across the Atlantic as the first notes of survival. On slave plantations, rhythmic work songs and spirituals encoded secret messages, offering hope and providing a means of escape. During the Civil Rights era, freedom songs galvanized movements and gave marchers the courage they needed to persevere. Blues is another Black music style that conveys emotions related to hardships and human struggle, and yet offers a sense of release from the pain. These were not just songs; they were soul-encoded signals of resistance and resilience.

African 6/8 rhythms, I-IV-V blues chords, jazz scat improvisations, and hip-hop looped beats are more than cultural expressions. They are sonic languages, harmonies, and rhythms of healing that tap into our collective consciousness. They connect us to our ancestral spirit and to one another. They remind us of who we are and who we can become. As in the Black expression, it is not what you say but how you say it. Reflects how your emotional tone and rhythms convey the meaning behind what is being stated and what is being heard.

Sound as Medicine for Trauma

Black people globally carry generational trauma mentally, spiritually, and physically. Much of this trauma lives not only in our minds but in our nervous systems. There is no single frequency that regulates the entire nervous system. However, specific frequencies, such as 528 Hz, have been shown to regulate the nervous system, shift brainwave activity, and reduce stress hormones, including cortisol.

From a scientific standpoint, resonance techniques, such as binaural beats, can also help regulate the body's responses to trauma. When two distinct tones are listened to in each ear, a third tone known as a binaural beat is produced. They are a type of auditory illusion that can help people relax, be more creative, and concentrate. In each ear, two tones with marginally differing frequencies are played. The difference between the two tones is the third tone that the brain senses. For instance, you will hear a binaural beat of 96 Hz if you hear 432 Hz in one ear and 528 Hz in the other. That is what separates the two. When properly embedded, these binaural beats have been proven to induce and improve states of consciousness. For Black people, this form of healing is a reconnection with ancestral strength.

Trauma Lives in the Body and So Does Sound

The Black community has endured generational trauma that lives in the body: hypertension, anxiety, fatigue, and grief. Western medicine often isolates illness in the physical body, but holistic traditions, many of which are rooted in African thought, understand that healing must occur on the energetic level. Sound, especially intentional sound, travels through the body, realigning frequencies, restoring balance, and soothing the nervous system.

Humming and toning can activate the parasympathetic nervous system, signaling safety and rest. Toning is the practice of using one's own voice to create sustained, single-note sounds to promote relaxation, stress reduction, and energetic balancing. This is especially vital for Black people navigating daily racial stress. The resonance of the healing sound of humming and toning can lower cortisol levels, regulate heartbeats, and open spiritual channels.

The Science Backs the Spirit

Modern research supports what our ancestors knew intuitively: sound has healing properties. Research indicates that sound therapy can improve mood, reduce stress, and enhance overall well-being. Frequencies like 432 Hz and 528 Hz have been shown to promote relaxation and cellular regeneration. Instruments like metal bowls, tuning forks, and African drums emit vibrations that entrain the brain into meditative states.

Yet, for the Black community, science alone is not enough. What makes sound healing powerful is the cultural context, the familiar cadence of a grandmother's hum, the communal echo of a Sunday choir, or the grounding pulse of a djembe. These are not only therapeutic tools; they are identity-affirming and soul-restoring.

The Power of Our Voices

Healing does not require external authority. The Black voice, when used with intention, is a healing instrument. Whether chanting "asé," speaking affirmations, or singing spirituals, we reclaim power every time we use our voices. Sound affirms our humanity, reclaims our worth, and re-centers our place in the cosmos.

Many Black people today feel disembodied, separated from their voice, power, or rhythm. Reintroducing sound into our daily lives, whether through toning, drumming, praying, or meditative tones, can activate parts of ourselves we have forgotten. It brings us back into the body and restores harmony where there has been dissonance.

Reclaiming Sound as Sacred

Too often, modern life silences our inner voice. Noise pollution, media overload, and disconnection from our roots have dulled our spiritual ears. To heal, we must reclaim sound as a sacred thing. This involves creating spaces where sound is intentionally used in meditation, worship, community healing circles, and personal altar rituals.

We must also cultivate our voice. Whether through singing, chanting, or speaking affirmations, using our voice to create sound is one of the most powerful tools of healing we possess. Our voice carries our truth, our vibration, our medicine.

Why Now Matters More Than Ever

In a world full of noise, reclaiming sound as healing is a revolutionary act. Our communities are battling grief, injustice, identity loss, and over-stimulation. Intentional sound gives us access to stillness, to memory, to restoration. This chapter marks the beginning of a journey, one that offers not just ideas but practices that can realign the mind, body, and spirit for Black healing.

Using the vibrations, frequencies, and energies of sound, sound healing is a holistic therapeutic approach that enhances mental, emotional, and physical health. Sound therapy is an ancient technique that has been practiced for thousands of years by Black cultures worldwide. The method is based on the theory that different sound frequencies can have a beneficial impact on our body's energy centers, or chakras, and encourage balance and healing.

When sound healing employs musical instruments, these strategies typically employ sound in a nonmusical manner. Mantras and chants for meditation, rhythmic drumming, and striking bells and bowls to create vibrating, wave-like sounds are a few examples. Traditional instruments, chanting, and sound therapy are becoming increasingly common in the wellness practices of yoga instructors, meditation instructors, and other holistic wellness practitioners. Scientific research has demonstrated the potential benefits of the sounds and vibrations created by crystal and metal bowls, gongs, chimes, didgeridoos, wooden flutes, and hand drums on our consciousness and emotional state.

A Call to Pay Attention

To heal the Black community, we must return to sound, not just as entertainment, but as a sacred force. The healing power of sound is not abstract or distant; it is tangible and accessible. It is already within us, in our history, our music, our breath, and our bodies.

I had to transform into a musician who focused less on being entertaining and more on healing myself and sharing that healing vibe with others. In doing this, I am calmer and less concerned about how people like me or my music and more about how I or my music makes them feel.

Let this chapter be an invitation: to pay attention, to listen deeply, and to remember that we have always known how to heal ourselves through resonance and reverence. Let us return to the sound, not just to hear, but to heal.

CHAPTER TWO

ANCIENT AFRICAN SOUND HEALING PRACTICES

Long before Western medicine codified the concept of "sound therapy," African civilizations recognized that sound could balance energy, restore spiritual alignment, and promote healing to the body, mind, and soul. In ancient Egypt (Kemet), Nubia, and throughout West, East, and Southern Africa, sound was more than a cultural phenomenon; it was cosmological. It was not simply art, but science. Not simply expression, but transformation.

I have been fortunate to travel and visit many African countries, including Nigeria, Ghana, Egypt, Tanzania, Kenya, Rwanda, Mauritius, Zambia, Botswana, and Mozambique. These travels have given me a deeper personal understanding of what it means to be African. Hearing the languages, learning customs, and performing music with the people of these countries has helped me bridge this knowledge to my work as a sound therapist for the Black community.

Sound as Sacred Science in Kemet

Sound healing in ancient Kemet and other parts of Africa was a profoundly spiritual, medical, and cosmic practice. It was not viewed as an entertainment; it was sacred science, integrated into rituals, medicine, architecture, and daily life. The Kemetic worldview understood that sound is a form of vibration, and vibration is a manifestation of life.

In the temples of ancient Kemet, the spoken word was considered *hekau*, a divine utterance, or word of power. These were not just affirmations; they were sacred vibrations intentionally shaped to alter reality. Priests and healers would chant sacred names and syllables in specific tonal frequencies to activate energy centers within the body and to align with *Ma'at*, the principle of universal order and balance.

The architecture of temples was also a part of the healing process. Structures were designed with geometric acoustics that amplified and carried sound in ways that heightened its spiritual effect. Kemetic mystics believe that all life originates from sound waves. In essence, matter, energy, and sound were all the same to the ancients. The King's Chamber, a part of the Great Pyramid in Giza, has a remarkable reverberation quality that was discovered during acoustic research, indicating that Kemet architects were aware of acoustics and incorporated it into the design. Given that Kemet was a spiritual location, it is reasonable to assume that the chanting and meditation techniques were intended to produce spiritual vibrations. By serving as electromagnetic energy concentrators, the stone selection enhances the power of sacred sites.

When the names of the *Neteru*, divine principles such as Ra, Asar (also known as Asr), and Heru (also known as Hathor) were spoken or sung, it was not merely symbolic. It was a sonic technology designed to harmonize the human body with the cosmos' frequencies.

Even tones like "OM" (also known as AUM), "SHU," or "RA" were not borrowed from other cultures; instead, they arose from shared ancient African systems of vibration. Each tone served a purpose: one to stimulate the pineal gland, another to cleanse the heart, another to awaken spiritual memory. In this worldview, sound was considered a form of light, and light was seen as a manifestation of life.

The Ankh as a Sound Healing Device

The ankh is a sacred instrument for channeling and manipulating frequencies, much like tuning forks are used to direct sound for therapeutic purposes. According to spiritual tradition, the ankh possesses specific frequencies that can be utilized in ceremonies to balance energy, transform trauma, and promote well-being. Kemetic healing techniques relied heavily on sound, including chants and magical words that contained vibrational frequencies. It is believed that the ankh was used to regulate and enhance these processes.

The ankh, as a healing instrument in Kemet, is believed to have been used to channel or direct energy and sound, balancing and healing the body and soul. Rituals can be used to activate the ankh's related frequencies, which can help cure ailments and transform trauma.

In modern sound healing techniques, a serene setting made with artifacts such as sacred objects can elicit peaceful vibrations and strengthen the connection with symbols like the ankh. After a ritual, the ankh's power is frequently activated and carried within the heart and energetic field, with its energy reverberating in one's actions rather than being confined to a tangible object. Through the synthesis of these forces, the ankh's sacred transmission and activation during a ceremony can awaken latent wisdom, bring forth soul codes, and restore one's inner self.

The Drum: Portal to the Spirit World

Across the African continent, the drum has long been regarded as one of the most powerful instruments for healing. It was never simply a musical tool; it was, and still is, a portal to our heartbeat. Instruments like the djembe, batá, dundun, and "talking drum" convey a rhythmic language that can communicate with the ancestors, the spirit realm, and the deepest parts of the self.

In Yoruba, Bantu, Akan, and other African traditions, drumming played a central role in ceremony and life transitions. It could induce trance states for spiritual healing, align the listener's heartbeat with the Earth's vibration, support collective rituals that released grief or celebrated joy, and even transmit coded messages between villages over long distances.

Each rhythm had its distinct intention and power. There were rhythms for birth and naming ceremonies, rhythms to guide souls through grief, rhythms to prepare for war, rhythms to call the rain, rhythms to welcome peace, and rhythms of resurrection. Drumming served as a means to process and release emotional trauma, activate joy, and integrate the individual's energy into the collective vibration of the community and the ancestors.

Call-and-Response: Collective Sonic Medicine

The tradition of call-and-response in African cultures is far more than a stylistic musical choice; it is a healing technology. It engages the body's parasympathetic nervous system, calms stress responses, and builds a deep sense of community coherence. This form invites each participant to be both a listener and a responder, reinforcing the truth that no one is alone in the circle.

In healing ceremonies, communal dances, and spiritual gatherings, call-and-response was a way for energy to flow back and forth, transforming both the caller and the responder. In Dogon trance rituals in Mali, the Bwiti healing ceremonies in Gabon, or the drumming traditions of the Ewe people in Ghana, this structure served as a sonic mirror, helping participants hear and reflect their spirit to themselves.

Instruments of Alignment

Beyond the drum, African sound healing traditions embraced a wide range of sacred instruments, each carefully crafted from the natural world to harmonize with the elements. The *mbira* or *kalimba*, a thumb piano originating from Zimbabwe, was used in ceremonies to communicate with the ancestors, its soft, metallic tones believed to bridge the worlds. The *shekere*, a beaded gourd instrument, carried both rhythm and water-sounds of cleansing vibrations, shaking away stagnant energies from people and spaces.

In Central and Southern Africa, the *Ngoma* drum ceremonies played a central role in curing illness, combining rhythm, chant, and dance in ways that treated the whole person—body, mind, and spirit. Wooden xylophones (balafons), harps (koras), and lyres accompanied oral medicine, storytelling, and initiation rites, reinforcing the teachings through rhythm and melody. Each instrument's materials, wood, gourd, and animal skin were chosen to connect the music-maker and the listener with the foundational forces of Earth, Water, Air, and Fire.

Chant, Hum, and Breath: Inner Tools of Healing

While instruments were powerful, African elders often taught that the most potent healing tool was the human voice. The hum served as a means to calm both mind and body, instilling thoughts and softening the heart. Chanting sacred phrases, they called divine energy into the space. Controlled breathing was seen as the direct channel of the spirit; *the breath was seen as the voice of God.*

Practices such as toning, moaning, and humming were intentional methods of vibrational release. They moved stuck energy, helped process grief, and transformed heavy emotion into resonance and light. Breath and voice were considered the first medicine long before herbs were gathered or hands were laid; the healer would work with sound.

Sound as Remembering

The Ghanaian Sankofa symbol is a bird that looks back to progress. This concept acknowledges the need to evaluate and build upon the past to achieve a prosperous future. Not based on material wealth but spiritual power and knowledge. In these dark times of hate and division, we must, especially as Blacks in the diaspora, look back to ancient Africa (Alkebulan) because we need as much wisdom as we can get to propel us forward.

For ancient African healers, sound was never used merely to alleviate a symptom; it was a process of reconnecting with the Self. To heal was to realign with nature, spirit, and one's lineage. Sound was the bridge between the living and the ancestral, the human and the divine.

In today's world of constant digital noise and disconnection, these ancient sound practices are not lost; they are waiting. When we reclaim them, we are not following a trend; we are returning to an inheritance. We are reactivating technologies encoded in our breath, our voice, and our spirit.

CHAPTER THREE

THE SCIENCE OF SOUND AND HEALING THE BLACK BODY

The notion of sound as medicine is grounded in tradition, intuition, and spiritual wisdom. Modern science is now acknowledging what African civilizations have known for millennia: sound alters the body. It moves through us not just as an aural transmission that we hear, but as sound, healing our mind, body, and spirit at the cellular level. It modifies our heart rate, breathing, brainwave patterns, and even our emotional chemistry.

The term "science" is derived from the Latin word "scientia," which means "knowledge" or to "know." It provides a foundation for understanding the physiological and neurological processes through which sound waves affect the body and mind. Science plays a crucial role in sound healing, as it supports the use of sound waves as a complementary therapy for relaxation, stress relief, and overall well-being. Quantifiable effects on brainwaves, heart rate variability, and the activation of the parasympathetic nervous system can result from external sound, encouraging the body's cells and energy fields to re-harmonize and re-balance. Scientific concepts such as vibration, resonance, and frequency entrainment explain this phenomenon.

Sound is a fundamental force that bridges the spiritual and material realms and is essential for communication, healing, and the transmission of information, according to research on sound from ancient Africa. With an emphasis on the spiritual resonance of sound and its capacity to convey meaning beyond mere auditory awareness, ancient Africans employed a variety of acoustic practices, such as chanting, toning, and the use of sound tools, for religious ceremonies, storytelling, and community building. Sound is a type of energy that propagates as waves through a medium, such as solids, liquids, or gases. Particles in the medium vibrate to produce these waves. A wave travels across the medium when an object or source vibrates, causing the surrounding particles to vibrate as well.

For the Black community whose collective body has endured centuries of stress, violence, and systemic oppression, sound offers a pathway to restore balance, release tension, and rebuild connection between physical, mental, and spiritual self.

Vibration: The Language of the Body

A holistic approach to good health, vibrational healing utilizes vibrations to enhance mental, emotional, and spiritual well-being. Its foundation is the conviction that all things in the cosmos, including the human body, vibrate at frequencies.

Vibration is the mechanical phenomenon of rapid back-and-forth motion (oscillation), about an equilibrium point. Vibrations are characterized by their frequency and amplitude. Everything in existence vibrates, and so do we. Our organs, our blood, our muscles, and even the fluids within our cells are in constant motion. Sound is simply a vibration that we can perceive through our ears, skin, and bones. When sound enters the body, it does not just stay in the ear canal—it travels through bone conduction and tissue resonance, shifting the frequencies within us.

In this way, a drumbeat does not just reach our ears; it shakes through our chest and spine. A moan or hum does not just create sound outside; it vibrates our rib cage, throat, and skull. These internal vibrations stimulate circulation, relax muscles, and activate healing responses.

For the Black body often holding layers of unprocessed grief and tension, this vibrational release can be profoundly therapeutic. It is the difference between bearing the pain in silence and letting the sound release it.

Healing Frequencies: 432 Hz and 528 Hz

Measured in Hertz (Hz), frequency is the number of sound wave cycles per second. In sound healing, not all vibrations are experienced equally. Two of the most respected tones are 432 Hz and 528 Hz, both celebrated for their restorative and balancing effects on the human body and spirit.

432 Hz: The Natural Resonance of the Universe

The 432 Hz frequency is often referred to as the "universal tuning" because it resonates closely with the natural patterns found in the vibrations of the Earth, water, and even the human body. Listening to music tuned to 432 Hz tends to feel softer, warmer, and more harmonious. Many people describe it as calming the nervous system, lowering stress, and promoting emotional balance. In essence, it draws the listener back into alignment with the natural rhythms. There is much debate between the 440 Hz and 432 Hz; some claim that the 440 Hz sound can cause anxiety and be toxic or harmful. Possibly, the 440 Hz became the standard international tuning because it divided people against one another and prevented them from being in harmony with each other.

Although there is no scientific evidence to support the assertion that 440 Hz was selected to induce "psychosocial agitation" or "emotional distress" to manipulate populations, it is believed that individual preferences for various pitches are entirely subjective. Just because there is no evidence to support the claim that the Rockefeller Foundation colluded with the

Nazis to use a pitch standard for financial gain makes me wonder why 440 Hz is the standard tuning.

528 Hz: The Frequency of Love and DNA Repair

Known as the "Love Frequency," 528 Hz is said to have a profound effect on cellular healing. By tuning the "A" pitch to 440 or to 444 Hz, the middle "C" will be at 528 Hz. Research in sound therapy suggests that this frequency may support DNA repair, reduce cortisol levels (a stress hormone), and promote an open heart to compassion and forgiveness. It is deeply associated with transformation, miracles, and inner harmony.

Either 432 Hz or 528 Hz can provide not only beautiful sound but also healing resonance. While modern instruments are often tuned to an "A" pitch at 440 Hz, shifting to these alternative tunings allows music to work more deeply on the body, mind, and spirit, creating a vibrational medicine that restores balance and awakens higher states of consciousness.

Solfeggio Frequencies

"Solfeggio" refers to the teaching of tones and notes through ear training, a term originating from music theory. According to sound therapists, the Solfeggio frequencies have a repeating pattern of six codes. The basis of these six codes can be reduced to the cross sums of 3, 6, and 9. The origin of the ancient Solfeggio scale can be traced to a medieval hymn and ancient Africa. Music has a mathematical resonance, and these frequencies were capable of inspiring humanity and the spirit of God. When the Solfeggio frequencies are played in sound therapy using tuning forks, they can affect healing on the mind and soul, and help put the body into a balanced state of movement. The following is a list of the original six Solfeggio frequencies and their healing attributes:

- 396 Hz: For liberation from guilt and fear
- 417 Hz: Undoing situations and simplifying change

- 528 Hz: Transformation miracles
- 639 Hz: Harmonizing relationships and inner balance
- 741 Hz: Living healthier and driving changes in lifestyle
- 852 Hz: Return to the mental and spiritual order

These are three further extensions of the Solfeggio frequencies:
- 174 Hz: Calming, grounding, and pain relief
- 285 Hz: Renewal of energy fields and rearrangement
- 963 Hz: Divinity, pineal glands, and spirit

The Nervous System and Sound Regulation

One of sound's most important effects is on the nervous system, especially the *vagus nerve*, which runs from the brainstem through the chest and into the abdomen. This nerve regulates our ability to calm down after stress and transition from "fight or flight" to "rest and repair."

Humming, toning, drumming, and slow rhythmic breathing all stimulate the vagus nerve. Using sound frequency to stimulate the vagus nerve can treat epilepsy and depression. For Black people who often live with chronic stress, whether from personal trauma or the constant vigilance required in racialized environments, sound healing can become a daily tool for resetting the nervous system.

Scientific research now confirms that low, steady tones, such as humming or toning, can help lower blood pressure and slow the heart rate. 432 Hz, 528 Hz, and binaural beats help synchronize brain activity, thereby reducing symptoms of anxiety and depression. Group chanting and drumming increase oxytocin, the hormone of trust and bonding. Our ancestors did not need a lab to know this; they intuitively were aware through lived experience that certain sounds "calm the spirit" and "heal our nervous system."

Brainwave Entrainment: The Mind on Sound

The technique of bringing two systems into harmony or making anything follow the same rhythm or pattern is known as entrainment. Brainwave patterns can be influenced by entrainment between the heart and brain, causing them to synchronize and oscillate at a similar frequency. The foundation of sound healing therapy for the human body is entrainment. Vibrating energies make up our bodies. Every sound is made up of some vibration.

The brain operates on electrical patterns called brainwaves. These patterns change depending on what we are doing and how we are feeling. The slowest and largest amplitude brain waves are delta Hz (1–4 Hz). Most noticeable when you are sleeping. It can facilitate the unconscious mind's access to information. The second slowest brain wave is theta Hz (4–8 Hz). Takes place during spiritual awareness, prayer, or meditation. These waves are linked to imagination, creativity, and intuition. When you are in a relaxed condition, as when you are awake but not actively thinking, you can detect alpha waves (8–14 Hz). These waves are associated with a reduced sense of discomfort and pain. The most prevalent brain waves in both adults and children are beta Hz (14–30 Hz), which might be associated with busy, agitated, or active thinking. The fastest brain waves, known as gamma Hz (30–100 Hz), are linked to concentration and higher-order brain processes.

- Delta (very slow) for deep sleep and regeneration [1-4 Hz].
- Theta (slow) for meditation, creativity, and emotional release [4-8 Hz].
- Alpha (moderate) for relaxed but alert focus [8-14 Hz].
- Beta (fast) for alert, problem-solving states [14-30 Hz].

- Gamma (fastest) for concentration and higher-order brain processes [30-100 Hz].

Sound, especially rhythm, can shift our brainwaves into these different states. For example, a slow, steady drumbeat at 3 to 6 beats per second can help bring the brain into the theta state, where deep healing, intuition, and emotional release occur.

This is why call-and-response chanting, repetitive affirmation mantras, and trance drumming are so effective; they change the brain's operating mode, allowing us to process emotions and connect with spirit in ways that words alone cannot.

Epigenetics and Generational Healing Through Sound

Trauma is not only stored in memory; it can also be stored in the body and passed down through generations via epigenetic changes. The emerging science of epigenetics shows that severe stress can alter gene expression, meaning the effects of trauma can be inherited even without the story being told.

For Black people, this means that the legacy of enslavement, displacement, and systemic violence may live in our DNA, influencing our stress responses, immune systems, and emotional regulation.

Sound offers a way to address this deeply rooted inheritance. Through vibration, we can begin to loosen the patterns of chronic tension. Create new neural pathways of safety and joy. Reinforce the body's sense of belonging and connection. When we breathe, hum, or sing together, we may be offering not just ourselves, but our entire lineage, a new pattern of resonance—one rooted in freedom rather than fear.

The Black Body as a Resonant Instrument

One of the most powerful truths of sound healing is that our bodies are instruments. The shape of our chest, the depth of our voice, and the length of our breath all influence the tones we can create.

Black voices have carried across plantations, filled churches to overflowing, and led movements for justice not because they were trained in a conservatory, but because they were rooted in necessity, spirit, and the pursuit of survival. This is not just a poetic truth; it is a physical one. The resonance of the Black voice, especially when liberated from shame and oppression, has a unique capacity to heal both the self and the community.

When we begin to think of ourselves as living sound instruments, we assume a new role: not just consumers of music, but also makers of medicine.

Sound as Everyday Medicine

You do not need a tuning fork, a sound bowl, or a drum to benefit from this science. The simplest tools are your breath, your voice, and your hands, which are always available. A few minutes of humming in the grandeur of the rising day, singing a gratitude chant, or tapping your thighs while sitting before bed, these are acts of both personal regulation and ancestral remembrance.

Many practices around the world are used to heal ourselves. Sufism, practiced in Northern Africa, is a system of beliefs, distinct from other religions. Yet, it is a school of experience centered on cultivating the heart and deepening awareness through the practice of prayer, meditation, and spiritual inquiry. Ancient practices, such as Sufism, Yoga, Tai Chi, and Qigong, are holistic healing systems that promote health and wellness.

Science confirms what our ancestors already knew: sound shifts us. It moves the spirit, rearranges the heaviness of stress, and makes room for love. It is unknown exactly how music affects feelings. Nevertheless, music has demonstrated throughout history and across cultural boundaries that it unites people, whether in prayer, conflict, romance, or the healing of wounded hearts. Scientists acknowledge that it is impossible to isolate the impact of sound on the body, brain, and emotions. Our physiology, psyche, and sense of self are all fundamentally influenced by sound and music. Our behavioral and cognitive abilities to adapt, survive, and procreate are influenced by music, as is the ability of mothers to soothe their infants, and perhaps most importantly, the ability to foster a sense of community. Many experts now believe that sound should be an interactive tool to be most effective as a therapeutic prescription. According to research, music making may change the brain. Because it promotes human welfare, music is at the pinnacle of the fine arts. Since the beginning of human history, sound has been used as a therapeutic tool, and many healers are also musicians. Sound and healing are intertwined in many African traditions. Research conducted in Ghana, Malawi, Zimbabwe, and other African countries has demonstrated how powerful music may change a person's mood. A healer can expel a spirit or disease in this altered state of consciousness, and sound, such as music, can serve as a protective measure against illness or an adverse event.

GUIDED PRACTICE
Sound Healing Ritual for Nervous System Regulation

Purpose: To calm the nervous system, release emotional tension, and reconnect with ancestral strength.

Time Needed: 10–15 minutes

Materials (Optional):
- Your voice
- Singing bowl or tuning fork
- Drum or small percussion (shaker, bell, or rattle)
- A glass of water (to symbolize flow)

Ritual Steps

Step 1: Ground and Breathe

Sit upright comfortably or lie down. Close your eyes.

Place your right hand on your chest over your heart, and your left hand on your belly.

Take five deep breaths: inhale through your nose and exhale through your mouth.

With each breath, whisper: "I am safe. I am whole. I am loved."

Step 2: Tone and Vibrate

Begin to hum gently. Let it vibrate in your chest and throat.

Try a low tone like "Mmmmmmmm" for 1 minute.

Feel the vibration move through your body.

This activates the vagus nerve and tells the body: *It's okay to be me.*

Step 3: Call on the Ancestors (optional)

Whisper: "I call on the wisdom of those who came before me.
May their strength return to my body.
May their songs live in my voice."

Begin softly chanting "OM... SHU... RA..."
Repeat slowly. Feel each word as a frequency, not a word.

- OM – the cosmic vibration
- SHU – breath, wind, spirit
- RA – light, energy, life force

Do this for 3–5 minutes.

Step 4: Listen

Now be still. Let the silence hold you.
Let your breath return to normal.
Feel how the body begins to recalibrate.

Step 5: Close with Gratitude

End with a hand over your heart. Whisper: "I am here. I am sound. I am healing."

Take a sip from the glass of water. Let it symbolize your renewed flow.

CHAPTER FOUR

THE ROLE OF THE DRUM IN BLACK LIBERATION AND HEALING

To the Black soul, the drum is not just an instrument; it is an inheritance. It is a heartbeat passed down from the ancestors, a code for survival, a call to remember. The drum has never just been about rhythm. It has always been about resonance with the body, with the spirit, and with the collective movement toward liberation and wholeness. It speaks to the Earth, to the spirit realm, and to the human heart. For African people and their descendants, the drum has been a heartbeat of identity, survival, and freedom. It has carried messages across villages, summoned warriors to protect the land, guided dancers into a trance, and sustained the rhythm for grief, praise, and protest.

To understand the drum in the context of the Black experience is to know that it has always been more than just rhythms. It is a tool of liberation, a spiritual medicine, and a technology of resistance. The origin of rhythm in Black people is both biological and cultural, rooted deeply in African cosmology, ancestral memory, and lived experience. Rhythm is not just a musical concept for Black people; it is a way of life, a spiritual language, and a survival tool.

From the villages of West Africa to the praise breaks in Southern Black churches, to protest marches on city streets, the drum has been the pulse of Black resistance, love, and spiritual repair.

The Drum as Voice of the Ancestors

In African cosmologies, the drum speaks. It is not simply played; it is conversed with. In Yoruba, Akan, and Mandé traditions, drums such as the talking drum (dùndún) were used to convey names, tell stories, and summon the ancestors. Specific rhythms were associated with orishas, ancestors, events, and ceremonies.

Across the African continent, every region and culture has its drumming traditions. In West Africa, the djembe of the Mendé people, the talking drum of the Yoruba, the Ewe's Kete and Agbada rhythms. Central Africa is home to the Ngoma drum, which is used in healing rituals and social ceremonies. Southern Africa has the Isigubu, kudu skin drums, and drum dances, which are used for celebrations and transitions. For North Africa, there are the bendirs, frame drums, and tar drums, which are integrated into spiritual and Sufi practices.

Each of these instruments carried not just sound, but also cosmology, a worldview. The drum was regarded as a sacred object, often crafted from animal skins and wood selected through a ritual process. It embodied the life force of the tree, the spirit of the animal, and the breath of the drummer. To play it was to enter a relationship with these forces.

Drummers were not performers. They were healers, historians, messengers, and spiritual leaders. To strike the drum was to invoke the spirit. To play, one had to open a portal. The rhythmic repetition brought people into trance states, where healing, prophecy, and spiritual transformation could occur. The drum has been and remains the bridge between the seen and unseen worlds.

Drumming in the Middle Passage and the Diaspora

During the transatlantic slave trade, enslaved Africans brought their drumming traditions to the Americas. Plantations, however, quickly became aware of the drum's power, not only for communication but for uprising. In places like the American South, slaveholders often banned drums, recognizing that a drumbeat could serve as a coded call to gather, escape, or revolt.

Yet, even when physical drums were taken away, African people found ways to keep the rhythm alive through body percussion, clapping games, work songs, and the stomping of feet. These adaptations were not just survival strategies; they were acts of cultural resistance, ensuring that the sonic memory of Africa could not be erased.

The Drum as Liberation Technology was Banned

When Africans were brought to the Americas in chains, one of the first things colonizers feared was the drum. In places like South Carolina, the Caribbean, and Brazil, enslavers banned drumming because it allowed enslaved Africans to communicate with the physical and the spiritual world. Fostered a sense of hope and courage, and conveyed messages of escape and freedom.

Starting in the early 18th century, African drums were outlawed in colonial cultures in North America, the Caribbean, and South America. Slave codes in the 1740s forbade the use of drums, as they considered them a harmful form of communication following the South Carolina Stono Rebellion in 1739. In Jamaica, colonial officials outlawed them during the early 1800s. Fearing that the traditional African drums used in Carnival festivities would spark rebellion, Trinidad & Tobago's colonial rulers outlawed them after the country gained independence in 1834. Enslaved Africans created alternative music and percussion styles, such as body percussion (like "hambone") and the use of other available materials, as a result of the bans, which showed their inventiveness.

The drum has always been a technology of liberation. In Maroon societies, communities of escaped enslaved Africans used drums to call meetings, warn of danger, and celebrate victories. The drum transmitted information faster than messengers could run.

During the Civil Rights and Black liberation movements of the 20th century, drums resurfaced as a visible and audible symbol of resistance. From Pan-African gatherings to political rallies, drummers reminded us that liberation is not only a legal or political act, but also a *spiritual vibration*. Even when the drum was outlawed, the rhythm never left. Black people clapped, stomped, patted juba, tapped, and booted. The body became the new drum. Resistance lived in the body's rhythms.

The Healing Power of Rhythm

From a physiological perspective, the drum works directly on the nervous system. The steady beat of a drum can entrain the brain's rhythms, guiding it into more relaxed or meditative states. Fast, polyrhythmic drumming can awaken energy, lift mood, and stimulate physical vitality.

In community settings, the effects are multiplied. When a group drums together, heart rates synchronize, breathing patterns align, and a shared emotional field emerges. This is why drum circles, whether in a village, a church, a protest march, or a healing workshop, are so powerful for the Black community. They reestablish the sense of collective heartbeat.

Throughout Black history, the drum has appeared wherever freedom was being fought for or reimagined, such as in the ring shout of Gullah-Geechee culture, characterized by rhythmic feet and hollers, serving as a form of spiritual resistance. Bambara and Yoruba rhythms were carried into Caribbean Vodou and Brazilian Candomblé rites. The Black (African American) church incorporated the drum into gospel music, creating soundscapes that lifted spirits and invoked joy. Hip hop transformed breakbeats into a form of protest, making the drum the backbone of a new Black language.

The drum helped us mourn. The drum helped us rise. The drum became a form of therapy for centuries of suppressed cries.

List of Popular Traditional African Rhythms

Abondan	A rhythm played for the king.
Fankani	Welcoming rhythm for important visitors.
Kakilambe	An important mask dance that appears only once a year.
Kassa	Is a harvest dance, which comes from the word meaning granary.
Kuku	Originally played when women come back from fishing.
Mendiani	Is a rhythm and dance for the virgins, the young girls from age six to thirteen.

The Drum in Modern Healing Work

Today, the drum is being reclaimed in the realms of wellness, education, and activism. Black therapists and healers use drumming in trauma recovery groups. Schools are reintroducing African drum classes to help restore cultural pride in young people. Activists bring drums to marches, knowing they can sustain morale and unity over long hours.

Even in one-on-one work, the drum can help an individual process grief, reconnect with their body, and feel safe enough to express emotions that have been buried for years. In a world that often seeks to mute Black voices, the drum insists: *We are here. We are many. We are powerful.*

The drum serves as a reminder that liberation is not just political, but also vibrational. When we drum, we connect with those who resisted before us, and we prepare the ground for those who will resist after us.

The Drum and the Black Body

Drumming is not just for the ears; it is for the nervous system. Science now confirms what our ancestors knew intuitively: repetitive rhythms can regulate heart rate, slow breathing, reduce cortisol (a stress hormone), and induce a meditative state of mind.

The sound of the drum is frequently connected to the heartbeat, and it is believed to have a body, skin, head, and voice. Both the drum and the human body are referred to as "beating bodies" and are connected by the skin, which is the body's primary sensory organ. The semi-permeable barrier of the skin serves as a communication tool, like the drum, in addition to helping with everyday tasks and providing protection from the environment. The drum's speech is like our own, and its beating is an extension of the beating we endure on our bodies. The skin serves as a conduit between the inner and outward worlds, whereas the drum serves as a conduit between the spiritual and material realms. Rhythm plays a significant role in how we perceive our body and the outside world.

The Drum and the Human Heartbeat

African drums represent the human heartbeat because of their rhythmic pounding, which evokes the heart's natural rhythm and helps people feel more connected to the Earth, their community, and themselves. The drum's historical use in uniting people for rituals, dialogue, and grief strengthens this close bond by fostering a common experience that reflects the basic rhythm of existence.

Physiologically like a human heartbeat, the constant beat of a drum evokes feelings of familiarity and comfort, particularly when it triggers memories of the sounds of the womb. The rhythm of the drum is a potent instrument for gathering people for various occasions and building a community's sense of cohesion, purpose, and identity. Since drumbeats are said to convey messages and act as a link between the material and spiritual realms, they are used as a tool for connecting with ancestors and communicating with the spiritual realm. The rhythm of the drum can also represent the Earth's and nature's pulse, reaffirming the notion that all living things are interrelated. Whether you are trained or not, drumming is innate. The body remembers.

The Drum as Communal Medicine

In Black culture, healing has never been a solo act. We heal in circles. We heal in rhythm. Group drumming reminds us: *I am not alone. I am part of something ancient, alive, and vibrating with power.*

Drum circles, ancestral ceremonies, and even casual jam sessions can create somatic resonance, a state in which bodies begin to entrain and regulate in harmony with one another. In these sacred spaces, drumming becomes a grief release, a celebration, a testimony, an ancestral invocation, and a visionary prayer.

The Piano as Part of the Drum Family

I am a pianist, but the piano is a part of the drum family. Although most people think of the piano as a stringed instrument, it is also considered part of the percussion or drum family. When a pianist presses a key, a felt-covered hammer strikes a string, producing sound through impact rather than plucking or bowing. This hammer-striking action is essentially drumming on strings, which places the piano within the broader family of percussion instruments. In this way, the piano carries both the harmonic depth of strings and the rhythmic, percussive character of drums—bridging melody and rhythm in one instrument.

The piano has been my primary instrument throughout most of my life; however, over the last six years, I have spent time learning and playing the djembe drum. These drums use vibrating membranes, typically made of animal skin, to produce their sounds. Not all instruments that are referred to as drums belong to this category; slit gongs, often known as slit drums, are one example. The skin or membrane of the membranophone drums is tightly stretched over a frame. The sound and beat of drums are fundamental to many aspects of life in most of Africa. According to the Bambara people of Mali, the term "anke dje, anke be," which translates to "everyone gather together in peace" and describes the function of the drum, is the origin of the name "djembe." The Bambara language uses the verb "dje" to mean "gather," and the word "be" means "peace."

Reclaiming the Drum Today

Today, Black people are returning to the drum not just in music, but in medicine. Mental health practitioners are using drumming in trauma therapy. Wellness practitioners are leading sound circles rooted in African rhythm. Cultural healers are training youth in ancestral percussion as a form of identity repair.

To reclaim the drum is to reclaim the body. To reclaim the drum is to reclaim voice, connection, memory, and rhythm. For me, playing the djembe has been a key element in becoming a sound healer. I realized the drum's healing influence on me. So, I convinced two of my band members to form a group, Brothas of the Drum, to help us manage our emotional outbursts, promote drum circles in our community, and encourage other Black men to join us.

We are not just tapping skins. We are tapping purpose and meaning. Rhythm in Black people is ancestral, cultural, and embodied. It comes from the land, the spirit, and the soul. It is both a memory and a map. A code passed down, encrypted in the drum, the footstep, the heartbeat, and the voice. Or as poet Amiri Baraka once said: *The beat, the rhythm, the sound, that's our DNA speaking.*

Reflection Prompt:

When was the last time you felt rhythm move through your body, not just as music, but as memory?

How might playing the drum help you restore the part of yourself that's been silenced or forgotten?

Think of a time you felt the power of the drum, whether in a concert, a march, a church, or a circle. What did it awaken in you?

How can you bring that same energy into your daily life or community work?

GUIDED PRACTICE
Rhythm as Remembrance

Purpose: To release emotional tension, reconnect with ancestral power, and restore rhythm to the body and breath.

Time Needed: 10–20 minutes

Materials:
- A hand drum, djembe, frame drum, or anything with rhythm (even a table or your thighs)
- A quiet space (indoors or outdoors)
- Optional: candle, incense, glass of water, photo, or item representing your ancestors

Ritual Steps

Step 1: Create Your Sacred Space (2 minutes)
- Light a candle or incense.
- Place the ancestor item or photo in front of you.
- Sit comfortably on the floor or chair with the drum in your lap or in front of you.
- Close your eyes. Take three deep, grounding breaths.

Say aloud or whisper: "I honor the ones who came before me. I call upon their strength and memory. May this rhythm awaken what is true."

Step 2: Align Breath and Body (2 minutes)
- Begin softly tapping the center of your drum with open palms.
- Let your breath lead the rhythm:
  - Inhale deeply...
  - Exhale, and gently strike the drum.

No need for a pattern yet, breathe and tap. Feel the vibration move into your hands, your chest, your belly.

Step 3: Establish a Simple Pulse (3–5 minutes)

Find a steady rhythm. Something like:
Boom – Boom – Boom Boom – Boom
or
Tap – Pause – Tap – Tap – Pause

Let this rhythm repeat like a heartbeat. Feel your body sync with it. Keep your jaw relaxed, shoulders soft, and breath flowing.

As the rhythm stabilizes, begin to hum softly. Let the hum rise from your chest. Allow your voice to ride the drumbeat; this is your sound.

Step 4: Call and Response with the Ancestors (5 minutes)

Now, imagine drumming as conversation. Say their names. Call them in.

Speak: "To Nana. To Baba. To those I never knew. May this rhythm reach you. May it bring me home."

Drum four beats to call. Pause. Listen.
Drum eight beats in response. Hum. Pause.

Let the rhythm become a living dialogue.
You might want to cry, laugh, or feel warmth; let it flow.

Step 5: Close the Ritual (3 minutes)

Slow the rhythm down. Let your hands rest.
Place both palms flat on the drum. Feel the echo.

Speak: "I return to stillness with rhythm in my bones. I return to myself. I am whole. I am connected. I am free."

Blow out the candle. Drink from the glass of water, symbolizing restored flow. Sit in silence for one minute and notice how your body feels.

Optional Variations

- Perform this ritual with others in a circle, synchronizing your rhythms.
- Record your rhythm and listen during meditation or sleep.
- Use voice or clapping if you do not have a drum.

CHAPTER FIVE

SOUND OF THE VOICE IN THE BLACK CHURCH AND FAITH COMMUNITY

The Black Church is one of the most powerful sonic environments in the world. Within its walls, sound is not decoration; it is deliverance. From the moan of a deacon before prayer to the thunder of a praise break, the sounds of the Black church form a spiritual technology passed down through struggle and sustained by belief.

For centuries, the Black worship center has been a sanctuary of survival, resistance, and renewal. It has been the one place where our voices could rise without apology, where the fullness of our sound was welcomed, celebrated, and sanctified. In the sanctuary, sound is not background—it is the heartbeat of the worship experience. It moves the body, opens the heart, and creates space for the spirit to descend.

In Black spirit life communities, sound is not confined to music alone. It is present in the hum of agreement, the rhythmic clap of hands, the swelling of a hymn, the call of the preacher, and the answering shout of the congregation. This soundscape is as much a healing environment as it is a place of praise.

Humming to Heal

Whenever I heard my mother humming in the kitchen while preparing dinner, it usually meant she was upset or bothered by something. Black people are carrying on the spiritual music tradition of humming, and our communities and ourselves are being healed by the vibration of our voices. People can benefit from humming to unwind, feel rested, and reset their nervous systems. Black people's voices are healing our communities and ourselves as we carry on the tradition of spiritual music. Humming is a technique that can help reset our nervous system, leaving us feeling calm and refreshed. Therefore, it gives us the impression that we are more comfortable and more relaxed in a church or faith setting, where we often find ourselves humming or listening to the hymns and hums coming from our neighbors. During sacred ceremonies, the congregation begins to hum and sway as the upbeat music shakes the room.

Sacred Sound's Healing Power

The deliberate use of sound, such as chanting, music, and vibration, for spiritual or therapeutic purposes or to strengthen a bond with the divine is known as sacred sound. Sound is regarded as a potent tool that can be used to harmonize the body and mind, create a sacred space, and cultivate consciousness in spiritual traditions worldwide. Between the spiritual and the physical, sacred sound can elevate the heart, soothe the nervous system, and strengthen our bond with God. The sound itself transcends language and heals the body and spirit, even in the presence of hallowed words.

The Church as a Sonic Sanctuary

In a world that tried to silence Black voices, the church became a space to be loud with the soul. The power of the Black church is not in its architecture; it is in its soundscape. Shouts, claps, foot stomps, organs, choirs, tambourines, all of it forms a sacred symphony.

The Black church acts as a "sonic sanctuary" by utilizing music and sound to create a safe, powerful, and restorative environment. In the face of structural difficulties and past trauma, the practice uses the church's acoustics as a potent tool for worship, resistance, and community building, offering comfort and joy.

Black people have been able to express themselves freely and find spiritual peace via music for generations, even when their bodies were not free. With its passionate gospel singing, energetic instrumentals, and hand clapping, the music uses vibration to "vibrate your soul," providing a profound emotional and physical purification. It is regarded as a type of spiritual healing that calms the body, mind, and soul.

Scripture from the Bible, including Psalm 100:2, exhorts people to serve God joyfully and approach him in song. This custom of "making a joyful noise" is frequently embodied in the Black church through spontaneous music, rhythmic worship, and call-and-response, all of which combine to provide a vibrant and spiritually charged environment.

People feel liberated and uplifted by the power of music, which brings a sense of rebirth and rejuvenation. Particularly for those in underprivileged groups who frequently feel powerless, the group singing and music transform into a potent, social experience that promotes joy.

This sound is a vibrational refuge. It says: "You are not alone. Your voice matters. Your tears are holy. Your joy is divine."

The Power of the Preacher's Voice

In many Black church or faith traditions, the sermon is not a lecture; it is a *living performance of sound*. The preacher's cadence, pauses, and rhythmic inflections are intentional, designed to move the spirit as much as the mind. The *whoop*, a melodic chant-like used in the sermon, becomes a musical bridge between spoken word and song, shifting the atmosphere and signaling the presence of the divine. This preaching method in Black churches, often referred to as "whooping" or "hooping," is characterized by the preacher's voice taking on a melodic, rhythmic, and musical quality, frequently featuring extended syllables that can lead to singing. This potent oral communication technique, which dates to the time of Black enslavement, utilizes improvisation and a call-and-response relationship with the audience to convey the sermon's message. It moves from conversational speech to a peak of emotion and tone.

Sound as spiritual technology, as in the preacher's voice, does more than share information—it works on the nervous system, inspires courage, and stirs memory. Many recall how the tone of a preacher's call could draw tears, ignite hope, or strengthen resolve in the face of hardship.

I can testify to being moved by a preacher's voice just this year. Minister Imhotep Alkebulan, the lead minister for the Wo'se Community of the Sacred African Way in Sacramento, California, had a passionate and scholarly approach to sharing the Word of God (Amen-Ra) that inspired me to join the Wo'se Community. A faith-based community that I have been affiliated with for over four decades, but had never joined until recently. The minister's upbeat and humorous expressions moved me with the Spirit. Imhotep's ability to not only teach the sacred texts but also deliver the message through song ignited a resonance throughout my body, mind, and spirit.

Unifying through Call-and-Response

Call-and-response is a compositional approach in music that functions similarly to a dialogue. The "call" is a "phrase" of music, while the "answer" is another phrase of music. These phrases may be instrumental, vocal, or both. In traditional African music, which primarily used vocal renditions, the call-and-response style originated. For instance, you will instantly recognize the technique if you think of gospel music: the congregation or choir reacts when the pastor or song leader calls out or sings a line. In other musical genres, call-and-response serves as a means of direct communication with the audience and experimentation. For instance, some artists employ call-and-response to engage their audience during live performances.

Call-and-response is foundational in the Black church, echoing African traditions in which leader and community engage in a constant sonic dialogue. The pastor says, "Can I get a witness?" and the congregation answers back. The choir sings the lead line, and the audience sings it back stronger. This is not performance, it is participation.

In healing terms, call-and-response creates a shared vibrational field where every voice is essential. No one is passive. Everyone contributes to the collective rhythm of worship. This sonic exchange fosters unity, reinforces a sense of belonging, and enables the congregation to affirm one another's faith and resilience.

Music as Healing Balm

The music of the Black church, including spirituals, hymns, gospel, praise, and worship, has always served a dual purpose: ministering to the soul and tending to the wounds of life. Songs like "Precious Lord, Take My Hand" or "Falling in Love with Jesus" are not just melodies; they are testimonies.

Gospel music can shift emotional states almost instantly. A single note from the organ, a sudden key change, or the entrance of the choir can bring a congregation to tears or to its feet in celebration. Neuroscience now tells us that such musical moments release dopamine, serotonin, and oxytocin, lifting mood and deepening bonds, yet long before science validated it, the church already knew that "a song will get you through."

The Shout: Healing Through Movement and Sound

One of the most distinctive forms of sound healing in the Black church is "the shout." Originating from the ring shout traditions of enslaved Africans in the Americas, the modern-day church shout involves rhythmic clapping, stomping, singing, and sometimes a full-body dance in the Spirit.

The shout is a way to release built-up emotional energy. The syncopated handclaps and footwork, combined with the choir's driving rhythm, create a communal heartbeat. Participants often describe leaving the experience feeling lighter, freer, and more connected to God. In this way, the shout is both a praise practice and a somatic healing ritual.

Testimony and Spoken Healing

Another key sound practice in the Black spiritual community is the testimony service, where members share personal stories of struggle, perseverance, and divine intervention. Spoken in the presence of the congregation, these testimonies are themselves acts of healing. They transform private pain into collective encouragement, and through the act of speaking and being witnessed, they help release emotional weight.

Testimony is also an opportunity for the community to respond verbally and sonically with affirmations like "Amen," "preach," and "tell it." This affirming sound reinforces the idea that no one is alone in their journey.

Harmonies of Healing: The Power of the Black Choir

The Black choir is more than harmonies; it is a collective memory. It is a group of voices, singing through trauma, declaring freedom, invoking power. The restorative power of the Black sacred choir provides an emotional release through singing, fostering a sense of community resilience, preserving cultural heritage, and serving as a spiritual sanctuary against trauma and oppression. Choirs regulate the breath and heart rate of those singing and listening. Foster emotional and communal connection. Elevate consciousness through layered vibration.

Singing in harmony occurs when two or more people sing on different, complementary notes simultaneously to create a pleasing, cohesive sound that adds depth and texture to a song. The most popular vocal harmonies are based on diatonic harmony, which utilizes intervals such as thirds, fifths, and sixths to produce consonant, aesthetically pleasing sounds. Notes and chords in diatonic harmony originate from the same scale. Close harmony, which produces rich, complete vocal textures and sounds, and parallel harmony, in which voices move in the same direction at a set interval, are critical approaches.

Harmony is crucial to represent resonant frequencies that restore balance to the body and mind, which can be disrupted by illness or stress. The act of singing in harmony teaches us resonance—how to be in tune with others, even while holding our unique note. That's healing in action.

Sound and the Holy Ghost

In Pentecostal and Holiness traditions, sound plays a central role in spiritual activation. The tambourine, the organ swell, and the rising volume of praise all contribute to the embodied encounter with the divine.

Speaking in tongues, vocal praise, and dancing in the Spirit are vibrational gateways through which people often experience physical and emotional healing, even without direct "therapy" involvement. The sound, frequency, and belief collide to form an energetic reset.

Healing Through Song and Testimony

A song is typically a composition for one or more voices, either accompanied by musical instruments or by singing. A song is composed of rhythm, melody, and occasionally harmony, if music is composed of ordered sounds. The pulse or meter provided by the rhythm allows the music to start moving. A line or phrase that may be played on an instrument or sung is called a melody. To show one or more tonal sounds alongside the line, harmony may suggest that the melody is overlaid with additional voices or instruments. Songs can be unaccompanied or accompanied by musical instruments. Through a diverse range of songs, including cradle songs, songs of reflection, historical songs, fertility songs, and songs about death and mourning, African music has consistently translated life's experiences and the spiritual world into sound, thereby enhancing and celebrating life, as noted by many musicologists and scholars.

Commonly found in Black Pentecostal churches are their parishioners testifying. A testimony is usually a personal account of an individual's experience with God and their faith journey. Testimony service is also a healing ritual. When someone stands to speak their truth about surviving, loss, or breakthrough, and follows it with a song, something ancient is activated.

Speaking in tongues is also a form of testimony or praying in the heavenly language of the Spirit. Modern neuroscience explains how praying in tongues activates unique areas of the brain and supports mental and emotional health. When people pray in tongues, the frontal lobe activity decreases, while the brain's receptive area is lit up. Speaking in tongues differs from speaking normally because your brain does not control it. You are yielding the Holy Spirit, allowing God to speak through you. The experience of speaking in tongues not only affects your spirit, but it also blesses your brain and body. It helps relieve stress and anxiety. Boosts the immune system. And because the parietal lobe becomes active, it may help balance or strengthen weaker areas of the brain, thereby enhancing overall brain function. The entire church experience can become a healing practice, whether through singing or being in the spirit of the moment.

Sound as Protest and Prophecy

Spirituals like "Wade in the Water" or "Ain't Gonna Let Nobody Turn Me 'round" were not just songs; they were survival codes. Sung in the fields, they carried secret meanings. Sung in marches, they declared freedom. Sung today, they still have the energy of resistance and hope. Even now, the Black church sound remains prophetic, calling out injustice, proclaiming freedom, and reminding us of our identity.

Why the Black Church's Sound Still Matters

Even in an era where many connect spirituality to wellness practices outside of organized religion, the Black church's soundscape remains a vital source of healing for countless people. Whether it is a Sunday service, a revival, a funeral, or a choir rehearsal, the sounds of the Black church remind us that worship is not silent, it is embodied, vocal, and alive.

The traditions of call-and-response, the shout, the whoop, the gospel choir, and the communal testimony all point back to an ancient truth: sound is sacred, and in community, it can restore the soul.

The Black Church's Role Today

Through these changing times, the healing power of church sound should not be lost. It can evolve by forming gospel choirs in community centers. Have healing circles rooted in spiritual sound. Embracing African drums, ancestral rhythms, and sound baths in Black churches and developing worship centers as vibrational liberation spaces.

The sound of the church remains a gift. When we reclaim it, not just as performance, but as ancient ritual, we unlock a medicine that still lives in our DNA.

Reflection Prompt:

What sound from your childhood church experience still lives in your body?

Was it the speaking in tongues? The harmonies of the choir? The preacher's whopping and rhythmic cadence?

What healing did it bring, and what sound in you might still be waiting to rise?

GUIDED PRACTICE
Sanctuary in Sound

Purpose: To create a sacred space of release, renewal, and empowerment using the sound traditions of the Black church. This ritual can be done individually or in a group setting.

Time Needed: 20–30 minutes

Materials:
- A comfortable, open space to move and make sounds with your voice
- Optional: tambourine or percussion instrument; a piano or organ
- A journal for writing a reflection afterward

Step 1: Enter the Sanctuary (3 minutes)
1. Stand or sit comfortably. Close your eyes and take three deep breaths in through the nose, out through the mouth.
2. Imagine entering a sacred sanctuary where every sound you make is welcomed and revered.
3. Begin with a soft hum, letting it vibrate through your chest. Feel it settle your mind and body.

Step 2: Call-and-Response Affirmations (5 minutes)
1. Speak an affirmation aloud as the "caller," then answer yourself as the "responder." Examples:
   - *Call:* "I am a child of God!" *Response:* "Yes, I am!"
   - *Call:* "No weapon shall be formed against me..." *Response:* "Thanks be to God"
   - *Call*: "I've come this far by faith!" *Response*: "Leaning on the Lord!"

2. In a group, one person leads the call, while the others answer together.

3. Let the rhythm of the call-and-response build until the space feels alive with energy.

Step 3: The Healing Clap (5 minutes)

1. Begin a steady, syncopated clap, think gospel service rhythm.
2. With each clap, imagine releasing something heavy: stress, fear, anger, or grief.
3. If in a group, sync your claps until you feel a shared heartbeat in the room.
4. Add simple phrases between claps, such as "Thank You," "Hallelujah," or "Amen."

Step 4: The Personal Testimony (5–7 minutes)

1. Speak aloud one truth from your life that you survived, overcame, or are still moving through.
2. Begin softly, but let your voice rise as you claim your resilience.
3. After each testimony, respond with a phrase of affirmation (alone or from the group), such as "Asé!" or "That's right!" or "Keep going!"
4. If in a group, give each participant time to testify while others respond.

Step 5: The Shout of Release (5 minutes)

1. Transition into movement, stomp, sway, or dance in place as you clap.
2. Let your body follow the rhythm naturally, without worrying about how it looks.
3. If you feel led, let out a joyful shout, moan, or cry, whatever needs to leave your body.
4. Keep the rhythm going until you feel lighter, freer, and more open.

Step 6: The Benediction of Sound (2-3 minutes)

1. Gradually slow the clapping and movement. Return to the soft hum you began with.
2. Place one hand on your chest and one hand on your belly. Speak: "My voice is power. My rhythm is healing. My sound is sacred."
3. Take three slow breaths. End with a whispered "Amen" or another closing word that feels right for you.

Note:

This ritual can be expanded with live instruments, a choir, or even just a simple tambourine. The key is intention, bringing the same openness, passion, and Spirit-led energy of the Black church into a healing practice that can be done anywhere.

CHAPTER SIX

SOUND HEALING MODALITIES FOR TODAY'S BLACK HEALERS

Black people have always been healers through rhythm, song, word, and presence. Today, a new generation is reclaiming ancient sound practices and blending them with modern tools to restore our communities. Whether in barbershops, yoga studios, therapy rooms, or church basements, sound healing is evolving. But it remains grounded in the same truth: frequency and vibration are our medicine.

From the first stolen Africans who stepped onto foreign shores to the present-day struggles for equality, sound has been our weapon, our shield, and our rallying cry. The voices, chants, drums, and songs of Black protest movements have not only carried demands for justice, but also *our very survival*.

In the streets, sound is more than noise. It is a strategy. It coordinates movements, communicates without microphones, and sustains morale during long hours of resistance. And in the face of oppression, it becomes a declaration: We will not be silenced.

In every corner of our culture —from barbershops to Baptist pulpits, from kitchen humming to hip-hop cyphers —the Black community has always lived in sound. But as trauma compounds and modern life disconnects us from ourselves and each other, we are being called to reclaim sound as a healing modality intentionally.

This chapter presents practical and sound healing modalities for Black healers, artists, educators, and spiritual leaders who seek to integrate sonic wellness into their work. It will delve deeper into how today's Black healers, teachers, artists, and everyday individuals can utilize sound—not just as art or performance, but as a ritual, medicine, and a means of liberation.

The Ancestral Roots of Protest Sound

The sonic strategies of modern protests are deeply rooted in African tradition. In West Africa, talking drums were used to communicate between villages. Most African dialects are based on tonal sounds and can be expressed through the tonal sounds of a drum, such as the djembe, which uses three clear sounds: the bass, the tone, and the slap. In the Caribbean and the Americas, drum rhythms and call-and-response singing preserved this function under the watchful eyes of colonizers. These rhythms could signal meetings, warn of danger, or call a community to action.

During the enslavement period in the United States, the "invisible church" gatherings of people in bondage used spirituals both as worship and as resistance tools. Songs like "Follow the Drinking Gourd," "Swing Low, Sweet Chariot," or "Steal Away" carried double meanings, with praise on the surface and instructions for escape beneath. The sound was the code, and those who knew how to listen were guided toward freedom.

March as a Moving Choir

In the Civil Rights Movement, the protest march became a moving sanctuary. Freedom songs like "Ain't Gonna Let Nobody Turn Me Around" and "We Shall Overcome" served multiple purposes. They kept protesters in step, lifted morale in the face of violence, and they sent a sonic message of unity to onlookers and opponents alike. Even without amplification, a thousand voices singing together could be heard for blocks, reminding everyone within earshot that this was not just a crowd, but a movement.

These songs also regulated the nervous system. Marchers facing dogs, water hoses, and police batons could use singing to steady their breath, keep their minds clear, and remind themselves of their higher purpose.

Chant as Power, Not Just a Slogan

Modern protests often center around short, repeatable chants: "No justice, no peace!" "Black lives matter!" "Say her name!" These phrases are more than political slogans—they are mantras. Repeated over and over, they enter a rhythmic trance that strengthens resolve and keeps a crowd connected. The human brain is wired to synchronize to repeated sound, which means a chant not only unites the voices but also aligns the energy and intention of the people. In this way, a protest chant becomes both a spiritual affirmation and a battle cry.

The Drum in Protest

The drum remains a vital instrument of protest. In marches from Ferguson to Lagos, from Minneapolis to Port-au-Prince, drummers set the pace for movement and give the protest a heartbeat. The bass drum can be felt through the chest even when voices are hoarse, keeping the energy alive when the body is tired.

Drums are also disarmingly joyful. Even in tense situations, a drum circle can shift the mood from fear to courage, from despair to celebration of survival. This is not accidental, African diasporic traditions have always understood that joy is a form of resistance.

Sound as Collective Protection

In dangerous situations, sound can both protect and inspire. In some protests, coordinated chanting or singing has been used to drown out police orders meant to confuse or disperse a crowd. At other times, a sudden silence, an entire group going still and quiet at once, can disorient those who would harm them. This mastery of group sound dynamics is a living example of how protest movements use rhythm and volume as tactical tools.

The Healing Side of Protest Sound

While protests are designed to disrupt, the sound within them also has a healing effect. For participants, the very act of raising their voice against injustice can release stored tension and transform feelings of helplessness into a sense of agency. Singing in solidarity affirms that the struggle is shared and that the burden is lighter when carried together.

Even long after a march ends, the sound lingers in the body. Many describe hearing the chants in their dreams and feeling the drumbeats in their chest days later. This is the afterglow of protest sound; it rewrites the body's memory, replacing the image of oppression with the embodied memory of resistance.

Why We Must Keep Our Sound Alive

Oppressive systems have always sought to silence our voices, whether through laws banning drums, noise ordinances targeting gatherings, or violence aimed at breaking our will. But history shows us this: if there is breath in our bodies, there will be sound in our movements.

We must remember that every time we chant, sing, or drum in the streets, we are not only fighting for policy change, but we are also engaging in a ritual of liberation that ties us to our ancestors and prepares the way for our descendants.

Experiencing A Sound Bath

If you have never experienced a sound bath, especially one led by a Black Sound Therapist, you should give it a try. A sound bath is a meditative practice where you relax comfortably while a practitioner uses instruments such as singing bowls, gongs, and chimes to create deep, resonant sounds and vibrations. Having a sound bath performed by someone from your own culture makes it seem more personal.

A sound bath is akin to soaking in a bathtub filled with sound frequencies and vibrations. It calms you and feels very mystical, which makes you vibrate from the inside out. When you are there, lying on your yoga mat with your eyes closed, the sound envelops your body, making everything feel like the hot water in a tub. Cleansed and refreshed.

The Black Healer's Responsibility and Opportunity

Sound healing is not just about technique; it is about intention, vibration, and ancestral alignment. For the Black healer, it also carries cultural weight. We are not just treating the nervous system; we are tending to the soul wounds of our people.

A Black healer must ask. Am I grounded in my culture and tradition? Is this modality restoring my people or mimicking someone else's path? Can I adapt this practice without losing my cultural identity? We are not here to duplicate. We are here to re-member and revive.

Healing Rooted in Cultural Truth

The sound healing movement has become popular in wellness spaces, but much of it has been shaped by Western or Eastern models that often exclude the Black experience and history. Black people are not simply inserting ourselves into existing frameworks; we are reviving our legacy.

I have been engaged with a collective of holistic healers, Rondy "Chocolate Buddha" Isaac, and Coach Chris Rodriguez, who meet on Saturday mornings in Oakland, California, for what Rondy has framed as Barbershop Yoga for Black men. Chocolate Buddha leads these gatherings with yoga, Coach Chris steers the dance movement, and I (Doc T) conduct the sound bath. These sessions begin with a check-in, during which each participant shares how they are feeling and updates on what's happening in their current lives. As Black men, we need to bond together and release our traumas in wellness spaces that are rooted in African ritual ceremonies.

In African traditions, sound was always a tool for releasing grief, celebrating transitions, aligning with the spirit, and connecting across generations. Black healers today are reimagining how these ancient techniques and tools meet modern trauma, mental health, racial fatigue, and spiritual disconnection.

Let's explore how.

Six Core Sound Healing Modalities for Today's Black Healer

1. Vocal Liberation Work: The Voice as Healing Instrument

The most powerful sound tool you have is your voice. It is your most ancient healing instrument. No drum, bowl, or instrument holds as much resonance with your body and spirit as your natural voice.

Modalities:
- Chanting (e.g., "Fanga Alafia")
- Toning (sustained vowel sounds like "AHHH," "OOOH")

- Affirmation work
- Singing or moaning from the heart

Benefits:
- Regulates the vagus nerve
- Reconnects to ancestral sound memory
- Releases emotional tension
- Restores personal power

Example: Before leading a group session, begin with a call: "I am confident. I seek truth. I am forgiving." Invite the group to repeat and harmonize.

African people have been seeking healing through humming and moaning since arriving from the slave ships. Let's keep moving our sound forward for justice.

2. Ancestral Drumming and Rhythm Work
The drum never forgot who we are.

Drums are not just percussion; they are portals. Every beat reminds our bodies of the first rhythm we knew: the heartbeat. Rhythm is our root.

Materials:
- Djembe, frame drum, talking drum, cajón
- Agogo bells, shekere, tambourines
- Body percussion (clapping, stomping)

Practices:
- Heartbeat drumming: slow, steady rhythm for grounding
- Call-and-response drumming and chanting: one person leads, others echo
- Body percussion: stomping, clapping, patting for nervous system reset

- Ritual drumming for grief, joy, initiation, or release

Benefits:
- Grounds the body
- Builds group coherence
- Induces trance/healing states

Example: Begin each community circle with a 3-minute rhythm loop that mimics a heartbeat. Invite others to layer their rhythm over it. This entrains the group into unity and presence. *Where there is rhythm, there is remembering.*

3. Sound Bowls and Tuning Forks: Frequency Tools
When you can't talk it out, tone it out.

Sound tools, such as tuning forks, sound bowls, and chimes, create pure frequencies that can shift the body's energy field and emotional patterns. These tools create steady frequencies that bring the body into harmony.

Modalities:
- Crystal and Himalayan (steel) singing bowls (ideal for chakra and breath work)
- Tuning forks (used on or around the body)
- Bells or chimes to open and close the healing space

Integration Tips:
- Use sound bowls between breathwork or meditation cycles
- Apply tuning forks over the heart, forehead, or joints
- Pair with intention and affirmation

Example: Use a 528 Hz tuning fork over the heart center while affirming: "My heart is open. My body is safe." *Modern tools become ancient when activated with purpose.*

4. Liberation Singing and Sacred Song

We have always sung our survival.

Spirituals, gospel, protest chants, soul songs, our music was never just entertainment. It was a matter of survival, ceremony, and soul communication.

Practices:
- Sing or chant old spirituals with a new intention
- Create collective chants rooted in Black joy or protest
- Use improvisational "freedom singing" to release emotion

Examples:
- "Kumbaya, My Lord" is a spiritual grounding hymn
- "I am free," repeated to an improvised melody
- Circle song: One leads, others echo and harmonize

5. Sonic Meditation and Sound Baths

Silence becomes sacred when sound prepares you for calmness.

Stillness, when paired with intention and subtle sound, can be profound for Black folks navigating hypervigilance, grief, and burnout. Sound can be internal, imagined, or paired with breath and guided imagery.

Practices:
- Listening to healing frequencies (e.g., 432 Hz, 528 Hz)
- Guided meditation with ancestral soundscapes or drumming
- Low-volume bowls, bells, and breath tones
- Quiet toning followed by shared silence

Benefits:
- Enhances emotional regulation
- Supports trauma recovery

- Builds inner vision and intuition

Example: In a small circle, begin with 3 minutes of humming, 3 minutes of singing bowl tones, and 5 minutes of group silence—Journal what arises.

The inner ear is as sacred as the outer ear.

5. Community Sound Rituals
Healing is magnified in community.

Ideas:
- Weekly drum circles
- Faith-inspired sound baths
- Liberation affirmation sessions for Black youth
- Sacred sound nights with ancestral chants, testimony, and rhythm

When Black people make sound together, the ground remembers us.

6. Everyday Sound Rituals for Black Life
Make healing normal. Make it daily.

Sound healing doesn't always require ceremony. Build it into your life:
Ideas:
- Hum while cooking
- Say affirmations aloud in the car
- Play African uplifting music while cleaning
- Create a "sound altar" with bells, bowls, and water

A humming kitchen can be a temple. A handclap can be a blessing. A whispered name can be a libation.

Becoming a Sound Healer in Your Own Life
You do not need certification to start. You need:
- Integrity

- Cultural awareness
- Respect for ancestors and the power of vibration
- Love for your people

Begin where you are. With what you have. In your voice. Let it grow from there.

Healing Is Ongoing

Sound healing is not a one-time fix. It is a practice, a rhythm you return to.

You do not need to sound "pretty." You do not need a perfect pitch. You only need presence and a willingness to resonate with truth.

We are not performing.
We are reclaiming.
We are remembering.
We are vibrating back to ourselves.

Cultural Integrity Matters

Many sound healing spaces in the mainstream wellness world are rooted in Eastern or New Age traditions. Black healers must navigate with care:

- Avoid cultural appropriation, honor African and Black diasporic sounds and rhythms.
- Learn from elders and griots.
- Do not be afraid to create your protocols that reflect Black identity, spirituality, and soul.

We do not need to wear white robes and burn sage bundles to heal. A humming grandmother. A soul singer. A drummer at the cookout. These are our original sound therapists.

Reflection Prompt:

What modality from this chapter speaks to you most?

What sound practices already live in your life?

Which ones might you now claim intentionally, not as tradition, but as transformation?

What is the protest song, chant, or rhythm that has stayed with you the longest?

CHAPTER SEVEN

RECENTERING THE BLACK VOICE AND SONIC IDENTITY

The Black voice has always been a powerful force. It has sparked revolutions, soothed generations, and shaped the soundscape of the entire world. And yet, in a society built on controlling and silencing Black expression, our voices have been distorted, muted, or manipulated, not just socially, but spiritually. The human voice is the most intimate and personal instrument of sound we possess. It is the only instrument we carry from birth to death, the one that can never truly be separated from our body. For the Black community, the voice has been more than a means of communication; it has been a survival tool, a cultural archive, a protest weapon, and a sacred channel for spiritual expression.

Our voices have carried us through the deepest valleys and over the highest mountains. They have told our stories when no one else would. They have sung our grief when we could not speak it. They have called our ancestors by name and shouted for justice when silence was no longer an option. The Black voice, in all its tones and textures, is a living monument to resilience. To heal as a people, we must recenter not only our physical voices but also our sonic identity, our ancestral sound, our unique vibration, and our unfiltered truth.

The Voice as a Channel for Spirit

Across the African diaspora, the voice has consistently been recognized as a sacred instrument, capable of bridging the gap between the human and spiritual realms. In many African spiritual systems, sound produced by the voice is considered *audible breath*. Since breath itself is life, the voice becomes a direct expression of the divine energy within us.

In the Black worship center, this truth is still evident. When a singer begins a faith-based solo or a minister lifts into a melodic sermon cadence, there is a palpable shift in the room. The sound carries more than melody or words; it carries intention, prayer, and ancestral energy. Those who listen do not just hear the voice; they *feel* it in their soul.

Vocal Expression to Release Emotions

The body stores emotions, especially those that have been suppressed or silenced. For Black people living under systems that discourage full self-expression, the voice can become one of the few safe outlets to release emotions. Singing, humming, chanting, moaning, and even wailing are ways of moving energy that would otherwise remain trapped.

Think of the moans, grunts, and shouts heard in old spirituals, raw, unfiltered sounds that were less about "sounding pretty" and more about connecting with the *divine spirit*. These vocal expressions were often done communally, amplifying their impact. When a parishioner lets out a cry, others would join in, creating a sonic wave of collective releases.

The Physical Effects of the Voice in Healing

Science now confirms what our ancestors already knew: that vocal sound has direct physiological benefits. When we sing or hum, vibrations travel through the body's blood and into the vagus nerve, which helps regulate our heart rate, digestion, and emotional state. This stimulation can reduce stress, lower blood pressure, and improve immune function.

The act of sustained vocalizing also increases lung capacity and oxygenates the blood. For a people whose bodies have carried the trauma of oppression, these physical benefits are more than incidental; they are essential. Our voices help us breathe more deeply and live more fully.

Laughter as a Sound Frequency for Healing Black People

As a fifteen-year board member of the nationally recognized African American Male Education Network (A²MEND), I have come to understand the significance of laughter. When you work diligently at a mission in education dedicated to empowering Black male college students, it is essential to calm emotions through laughter. The former president of A²MEND, Herb English, has reinforced the meaning of laughing from the belly up for me. By inviting more laughter, whether through jokes or shared experiences, we can foster positive energy and counteract the low frequencies associated with stress and anger. Community-based laughter is an effective way to promote healing and build resilience, especially in the face of ongoing societal challenges. Actively seeking out laughter and joy is a way to "program" the body and mind for healing and well-being.

Laughter functions as a positive sound frequency, by establishing positive brain pathways linked to joy, encouraging the production of "feel-good" neurochemicals like dopamine and endorphins, lowering stress-inducing cortisol levels, and bolstering the immune system. Laughing has a positive effect because it can alter the body's energy and promote a state of well-being, helping to heal both the body and mind. This is especially crucial for Black communities, which face intense intergenerational trauma and stress.

The Voice as a Cultural Archive

The Black voice has preserved history that was never written down. Through oral tradition, spirituals, blues, jazz scatting, gospel runs, hip hop verses, and spoken word poetry, our voices have carried the memories of our people from one generation to the next. These vocal forms are not just entertainment; they are living archives, holding coded messages, moral teachings, and the spirit of resistance.

Even when stripped of instruments, the voice alone could hold the melody, rhythm, and emotion of a song. This ensured that our musical and cultural traditions could survive the displacement of pain, the suppression of African languages, and the attempts to erase our heritage.

Reclaiming the Voice from Oppression

Centuries of systemic racism have tried to control how Black people use their voices, telling us when to speak, how loudly, in what tone, and under what conditions. From being silenced in courtrooms to being punished for speaking African languages, there has been a long history of policing our sound.

Reclaiming the voice is an act of liberation. Speaking truth to power, singing our own songs, and telling our own stories in our own words is a direct rejection of that control. Every time we allow ourselves to speak, sing, or shout without fear, we undo a little more of the harm that was intended to silence us.

The Voice as Medicine for the Future

The healing power of the voice is not limited to the past; it is an ongoing resource for the future. We can use our voices to affirm our worth, to bless our children, to guide our communities, and to heal ourselves. Whether in a worship hall, at a protest rally, in a hospital, or in a quiet moment alone, the intentional use of sound can realign the body, lift the spirit, and remind us of our belonging.

When we speak with love, sing with conviction, or hum in meditation, we are not just making sound; we are transmitting energy. We are shaping the vibration of the spaces we inhabit and leaving behind a resonance that others can feel.

The Voice as Frequency and Freedom

Your voice is not just speech. It is a vibrational signature, as unique as your fingerprint. It is the sounding of your soul. The pitch and timbre of a voice are produced by a complicated interplay between a fundamental frequency and several harmonics, rather than by a single frequency. While the relative intensity of the harmonics gives the voice its distinctive quality, or timbre, the fundamental frequency, which is established by the rate of vocal fold vibration (measured in Hertz), demonstrates the overall pitch.

To put it briefly, your voice is a complicated acoustic signal composed of numerous related higher notes (harmonics) and an introductory note (the fundamental frequency). Your voice is distinct due to the blend of these frequencies.

When we speak, sing, moan, shout, or hum, we activate the vagus nerve, the throat chakra, which is how we express truth and alignment. And our ancestral line through vibration and tone memory. As you reclaim your voice, you reclaim your *power,* your *presence,* and your *place in the world.*

The Sonic Identity of Blackness

We have a sound: a timbre, a rhythm, a globally recognizable cadence. Our sonic identity has roots that run deeper than a single genre. It is a vibrational language. It contains pain, resistance, humor, wisdom, and joy. But colonization, assimilation, and trauma have disrupted our connection to that authentic sound. To restore our sonic identity means allowing ourselves to sound Black, speak Black, and sing Black, without apology.

Affirmations and Mantras Employ Sonic Identity

To synchronize the mind and body with a desired state or aim, mantras and affirmations utilize sound identity through repetitive vibrations. These auditory repetitions bypass conscious cognition to create a resonant experience through rhythm, frequency, and emotional resonance. Whether it's a personal belief in one's own value or a spiritual connection with a higher power, the end effect is a more deeply ingrained identity.

Using precise vibrations, mantras, and ancient, sacred sound formulas, one can tune the mind to a particular spiritual frequency often associated with divine forces. Mantras have a special vibratory effect because the Sanskrit language is constructed so that the sensation of making a sound is its own meaning. For example, it is claimed that the primal sound OM represents the very nature of creation. Mantras' particular rhythmic patterns, when repeated, synchronize the body to resonate with auspicious, heavenly energies. These energies are often considered more potent than an individual's inner, more minor vibrations.

By replacing undesirable "noise" with a more deliberate and focused frequency, repeating a mantra can cleanse the body. This process, which aligns a person's inner state with a strong, harmonious pattern, might be thought of as auditory entrainment. It is believed that mantras are "precise" instruments for connecting with the divine. The power of the original sound is acquired and modified by the practitioner through imitation and resonance with sacred sounds.

Affirmations likewise use sound repetition to retrain the mind's identity and promote positive self-beliefs, even though they are frequently based on spoken words rather than holy tones. Affirmations that are repeated create new acoustic patterns that fight old, limiting ideas, much like a mantra. This "self-talk" helps overcome the self-defeating inner monologue that can hinder one's progress.

Affirmations can associate sound phrases with pleasant emotional states, much like commercial jingles do when they evoke brand connections. By repeating affirmations such as "I am worthy," you fortify brain connections that support the mental perception of that empowering statement. You can give your internal story a fresh and consistent acoustic character by mentally or audibly repeating a pleasant phrase. The affirmation feels more genuine and ingrained due to the steady, rhythmic reinforcement, which helps you reframe your self-perception.

The individual can create affirmations, which are frequently very personal. Even though they might not have the same age-old spiritual significance as mantras, repeated usage of them produces a potent, customized "sonic logo" that strengthens the user's intended identity.

The sound of our sonic voices, whether in affirmations, mantras, or songs, is a recurring theme in the history of Black people. Familiar beat patterns, themes, or poems by a lead voice, followed by the collective response of voices, served as a link to the African captives throughout the Middle Passage. Throughout the Black experience, the idea of affirmations and mantras for healing has persisted. These sonic sounds come from the fields of laborers, the ships of slavery, the perilous castles of harshness, and the protest rights walkers. Africans voiced their feelings. These sonic voices were a mix of depressing, joyful, motivating, affectionate, and repulsive.

The Black voice is not just a tool for communication; it is a lifeline, a release, a prayer, and a protest all in one. It is the sound of survival and the voice of freedom. In learning to use our voices fully, without apology or restriction, we tap into one of the oldest and most potent forms of healing available to us. And as my mentor and teacher, Baba A. R. Fariduddin Fred Johnson reminds me, "as we speak, so we are."

Practices for Vocal Liberation

Here are a few ways we can begin to heal and restore the voice:

1. Intentional Humming

A daily hum for 3–5 minutes calms the nervous system and opens the throat.

2. Vocal Toning with Breath

Use vowel sounds like AH, OO, or OM on long breaths. Let the vibration settle in your chest and skull.

3. Affirmation with Emotion

Speak phrases like:

- "I have the right to be heard."
- "My voice is sacred."
- "I speak for those who couldn't."

Let yourself *feel* the words, not just say them.

4. Storytelling or Spoken Word

Tell your story, out loud. Record it. Please share it with someone. Practice being heard.

5. Throat and Jaw Tension Release

Massage the jaw, neck, and shoulders. Yawn. Sigh.
Let spontaneous sound arise.

Communal Voice Work

Black liberation has always been communal, and so is vocal healing. Singing together, chanting in a circle, testifying in a safe space, these are not only cultural expressions; they are collective medicine.

Vocal healing in groups:

- Builds belonging
- Regulates collective nervous systems
- Affirms each member's dignity and sound

When the village sings together, it remembers itself.

Beyond Speaking—Sounding the Spirit

Restoring the Black voice is not about "talking more." It is about sounding more truthful. Sometimes, this means:

- Wailing
- Moaning
- Laughing loudly
- Screaming safely
- Humming a song, you forgot you knew

This is not "therapy," this is *ancestral ritual* returning through the breath.

Reflection Prompt:

When were you first told to "tone it down"?

What sound in you has been waiting to rise?

What would happen if you permitted it to come through?

GUIDED PRACTICE
Unlocking your Voice

Purpose: To release vocal tension, reclaim the power of your unique sound, and reconnect with ancestral memory through intentional expression.

Time Needed: 15–20 minutes

Materials:
- Your voice
- A quiet space
- A glass of water
- A mirror
- A journal (optional)

Best Time: Early morning, before bed, or before performing, speaking, or engaging in spiritual practice.

Ritual Steps

Step 1: Set the Space (2 minutes)
Stand or sit comfortably.
Place your hand gently over your throat or chest.

Say aloud: "I honor the sound inside me. I give myself permission to speak, sing, cry, and hum. My voice is sacred. My voice is safe."

Take three deep breaths. Inhale through the nose. Exhale through the mouth with a soft sigh.

Step 2: Yawn, Sigh, and Stretch (2 minutes)
Begin with natural sounds:
- Stretch your arms overhead
- Let out a big yawn, and vocalize it

- Release a soft "ahhhhhhh…" like relief
- Roll your shoulders and massage your jaw gently

These movements create space for sound to emerge.

Step 3: Humming as Nervous System Reset (3 minutes)

Close your lips gently. Begin to hum softly.

Focus on the vibration, not volume.
Let the hum settle into your chest, sinuses, or forehead.

Try this pattern:
- Low hum for grounding
- Mid-tone hum for balance
- High hum for release

Alternate for 3–5 rounds.
Each hum = one complete breath cycle.

Step 4: Vowel Toning with Intention (5 minutes)

Use your breath to speak and stretch sound into the room.

Try:
- "AHHH" (for the heart)
- "OH" (for grounding)
- "EE" (for clarity)
- "OM" (for cosmic connection)

With each tone:
- Inhale deeply
- Release the tone with your whole body
- Let your face and jaw stay loose
- Imagine light vibrating through your voice

Do each vowel 3–4 times.

Step 5: Affirmations: Speak Your Truth Aloud (3 minutes)

Now, speak directly to yourself.

Say a series of truth statements with emotion and breath.

Try:
- "My voice is enough."
- "I speak with power."
- "I have nothing to hide."
- "I carry the sound of my people."

Speak slowly. Pause between each. Let the body react.

Step 6: Sing or Chant Mantras Freely (3–5 minutes)

If you're ready, let yourself sing, chant, or vocalize any melody or rhythm that comes up.

It can be a:
- Spiritual
- Moan
- Church tune
- Hummed a childhood song
- Invented chant

Do not judge. Let it rise from the belly, from the bones, from memory.

Step 7: Close and Reflect (2 minutes)

Place both hands over your heart or throat. Whisper: "I return to my true sound. My voice is home. My voice is free." Drink a few sips of water.

Optional: Journal about what came up or record it in a voice memo for reflection.

CHAPTER EIGHT

COLLECTIVE HEALING THROUGH SOUND IN THE COMMUNITY

Healing in the Black community has never been an individual pursuit. From the circle dances in West Africa to praise breaks in Black churches, from freedom songs in the Civil Rights Movement to cipher circles in hip-hop culture, Black people have always found healing together. Through collective sound, we grieve, remember, celebrate, and rise.

A community is a collection of individuals who share a common identity, interest, or place of residence, which fosters a sense of cohesion and belonging. This term applies to both professional associations and genealogical groups. For me, the term conjures up two essential ideas: unity and common. Thus, when I refer to the "Black community," I mean a group of people who interact with one another and share similar ideals. The Zulu word "ubuntu" refers to a philosophical idea from Southern African cultures, often translated as "I am because we are" or "humanity towards others," that emphasizes the interconnectedness of people and communities. In essence, it is a set of principles and behaviors that individuals of African heritage or descent believe are essential to being a fully human being.

As I pursued a career as a sound therapist, one of my primary goals was to establish a community of Black sound healers and a collective of holistic practitioners. I am very fortunate to work with a fabulous sista who shares many of my views and perspectives on doing this work. Fatimah Hanif is genuinely a godsend, challenging me not only to heal others but also to continue healing myself.

Sound is communal medicine. It moves through us like breath, connecting us, calibrating us, and drawing us back into rhythm with one another. As trauma isolates, sound gathers. As silence stifles, sound frees. Sound has always been a communal aspect of Black culture. From African drum circles to neighborhood block parties, from gospel choirs to protest chants, we have used collective sound to create safety, connection, and transformation.

As we confront ongoing trauma, systemic racism, violence, poverty, and spiritual disconnection, healing in isolation is not enough. We need sound-centered community practices that restore harmony not just within individuals, but across entire families, congregations, and neighborhoods.

This chapter is a call to rebuild sacred sound spaces, spaces where our people can grieve, celebrate, and grow through the power of vibration, rhythm, and shared resonance.

Why Collective Sound Heals Differently

When we join our voices or our rhythms, something profound happens; our bodies and minds begin to synchronize. Science refers to this phenomenon as entrainment: heartbeats align, breathing patterns synchronize, and brainwaves shift into the same frequencies. In those moments, we are not just individuals; we are one body, one heartbeat, one vibration. This shared state builds trust and safety, which are essential for deep healing. For Black communities who have carried generations of trauma, isolation, and displacement, this shared vibration can be a lifeline, a way of remembering that we belong, that we are seen, and that we are not alone.

Individual sound healing can relax the body and open the spirit. But in group participation, sound amplifies healing through the convergence of multiple voices, creating resonance fields that entrain the nervous system. Group drumming synchronizes heartbeats and breathing patterns. Communal chants build coherence, reminding us that we are not alone.

Scientific studies have shown that group singing increases oxytocin (the hormone associated with bonding). Rhythmic synchronization increases empathy and trust. Collective vocalization reduces symptoms of depression and anxiety. But long before science, we knew this truth: *When we sing together, something in us becomes whole again.*

Community Sound Heals Deeper

In many African traditions, sound was never meant to be a performance. It was a ritual act, a means to maintain harmony among themselves and with the natural world. Everyone participated, regardless of skill. The beauty of the sound came from the unity of the group, not the perfection of the individual. This ethos traveled with our ancestors across the ocean and found new forms in the ring shout, the call-and-response, the protest chant, and the gospel choir. Even today, in a crowded church or at a rally in the streets, the collective sound carries the same ancient power—it moves energy, clears grief, and calls forth joy.

Individual healing practices are essential, but they cannot replace the power of being witnessed and held in collective sound. When we sing or drum in community, we are reminded that we are not alone. We become part of a larger vibrational field that supports regulation and release. Our voice contributes to a sound that is greater than the sum of its parts.

In group settings, what one person cannot release alone, the community can release together. That is the spiritual physics of rhythm. This is why so many of our ancestral healing traditions are built around circles: drumming circles, dance rings, testimony services, cipher battles, and even family cookout jams. These are not just cultural; they are communal calibrations.

Ritual, Not Performance

One of the most significant shifts we must make in modern wellness spaces is to return sound to its ritual roots, rather than just focusing on performance. In too many spaces, sound has become something we consume rather than something we co-create. But in collective healing, participation is more important than perfection.

We must remind each other that your singing does not have to sound perfect. You do not need a good voice; you need your breath and your presence. Whether it is a moan in a grief circle or a stomp in a protest march, the intention behind the sound is the medicine.

Reclaiming Our Sonic Gathering Spaces

Colonialism and systemic oppression tried to strip us of these sonic gathering spaces. Laws banning drums, noise ordinances in Black neighborhoods, and the destruction of cultural meeting places all aimed to disrupt our ability to heal together. Yet the legacy of collective sound endured. We adapted by turning to the body itself as an instrument, clapping, stomping, patting juba, and using our voices to keep the rhythm alive. These adaptations were not just survival strategies; they were acts of resistance, ensuring that the communal heartbeat could not be silenced.

Racism and oppression disrupted many of our traditional sound spaces. Noise ordinances, gentrification, and institutional suppression have robbed us of our right to gather in rhythm. But the legacy is still alive. And it is ready to return.

We can reclaim and rebuild healing circles in community centers, drum sessions in the park. Develop intergenerational story-and-song gatherings. Bring back kitchen table humming rituals, and sound healing nights in barbershops, churches, mosques, and rec rooms. Sound is *our birthright*. And it is space that turns it sacred.

Collective Sound as Resistance

Sound in the community is more than a pleasant experience; it is a force that can transform the emotional climate of an entire group. When one person in a circle begins to sing or hum, others join in. The melody builds, weaving itself into the room until everyone is carried by it. In this shared vibration, pain feels lighter, hope feels nearer, and the burdens we carry alone begin to dissolve in the presence of many. For someone who feels unseen or unheard in the world, having their voice rise and merge with others can be deeply restorative. It says, without words, "You belong here. Your voice matters."

In moments of protest and uprising, collective sound becomes a shield, a weapon, and a sanctuary. The chants. The claps. The songs passed through generations. They do not just raise morale, they raise power.

When we chant "People Get Ready!" in the streets or "Ain't No Stopping Us Now" at a rally, we are not just calling for justice; we are calling in our ancestors. We are harmonizing our will, aligning our breath, and amplifying our demand for liberation. In this way, sound is not only healing. It is a strategy.

Sound Is a Mirror of the Village

Collective sound is also a tool for liberation. Throughout history, Black people have used music and rhythm not only to heal but to organize, strategize, and resist oppression. From the coded messages in spirituals to the freedom songs of the Civil Rights Movement, our communal sound has been a rallying force, aligning bodies and minds toward a common goal. Even in times of celebration, the rhythm has carried the memory of survival and the vision of freedom forward. Joy itself becomes a radical act, a declaration that we are still here, still whole, still capable of beauty.

I grew up in a Black, close-knit community, Parchester Village, in Richmond, California. In the mid-to-late 1960s, the Black Panthers would meet in a storefront building to hold their meetings. When members of the Panthers met, some would often be positioned out front of the space, playing their conga drums. I later learned that if the drummers stopped, the delegates inside would recognize a problem and discontinue their discussions. Both sound and silence are used as tools for liberation.

When we hear each other, we see each other. The collective sound makes us audible to ourselves again. It breaks the trance of isolation. It restores the drumline of belonging. And most importantly, it offers joy.

In spaces where we often manage grief, code-switch, or survive in white spaces, a drum circle, a gospel harmony, or a dance cypher becomes an act of radical restoration. The sound tells us: "You are present." "You are beautiful." "You are connected to the ancestors." "You are Black and Proud."

The Sacred Science of Sound Togetherness

Today, reclaiming our right to gather in sound is part of reclaiming our wholeness. This can happen in many ways, drumming in a public park, holding intergenerational song circles in community centers, hosting sound healing nights in churches or barbershops, or simply gathering family members to hum, clap, and sing together after a shared meal. The space does not have to be formal; it just needs to be intentional. The power comes from the collective intention to use sound as a bridge between hearts, a salve for old wounds, and a reminder that our strength has always been in our togetherness.

Scientific studies have shown that collective rhythm and vocalization can synchronize breathing and heart rates. Increase oxytocin levels, reduce cortisol, and foster feelings of empathy, connection, and belonging. However, long before science began measuring these effects, Black communities had known this intuitively. When a mother starts humming and her children calm down, when a congregation sings as one and grief breaks into joy, when the beat drops and the whole crowd nods in time, these are moments of healing. Energetic recalibrations. Sound is more than expression; it is a tuning fork for the village nervous system.

The Loss of Sonic Gathering Spaces

In a time when so much seeks to divide and isolate us, collective sound offers an antidote. It returns us to the truth that healing is not just a personal act, it is a communal responsibility and a communal gift. When we lift our voices or our drums together, we are not simply making music; we are aligning our spirits, mending the invisible threads between us, and creating a vibration strong enough to carry us all forward. In that moment, we are not separate—we are the village.

Indeed, music is a fundamental aspect of humanity and may impart a wealth of life lessons. Music creates community because it unites people daily. We are unable to turn off our hearing, which is arguably our strongest sense. Continue to perform and join the global orchestra of sound.

Colonialism and imperialism have eroded many Black communities' sound spaces that had African drumming banned during the period of enslavement in America and labeled public singing and testifying as disruptive. Policed and silenced Black neighborhoods as noise pollution. And removed healing sounds from schools and public life. What remains are fragments, church choirs, cipher circles, kitchen-table harmonies. But we can rebuild these spaces on our terms.

Building Sonic Healing Communities Today

1. The Healing Circle

A sacred container of voice, breath, rhythm, and listening.

Elements:

- A central drum or altar
- Grounding breath and hum
- Rotating vocal offerings (moans, words, chants)
- Shared rhythm and rest

Ideal For: grief support, spiritual realignment, intergenerational healing

2. Community Drum Sessions

Gatherings rooted in ancestral rhythm.

Elements:

- African drums, shakers, and body percussion
- Call-and-response patterns
- Spontaneous movement or dance
- Closing silence and gratitude

Ideal For: youth programs, neighborhood healing, liberation events

3. Sonic Meditation in Black Spaces

Intentional silence, sound, and presence.\

Elements:

- Tuning forks or singing bowls
- Breath and low hum
- Vocal affirmations spoken together
- Shared journaling or testimony

Ideal For: wellness retreats, Black men's or women's groups, spiritual space

4. Liberation Chant and Protest Song

Sound as action and resistance.

Elements:

- Communal callouts ("Power to the People!" "No Justice, No Peace!")
- Rhythmic foot stomps and claps
- Reclaimed spirituals and cultural chants
- Drumming for marches or vigils

Ideal For: activist spaces, community justice movements

Sound Belongs to the People

You do not need a music degree or wellness certification to create sonic healing spaces.

What you need is:

- Intention
- Respect for ancestral practice
- An open heart
- The willingness to listen, sound, and hold space together.

Whether it is an evening toning meditation, a family prayer circle, or a block party with a drumline, these are sacred. They are already healing us.

Reflection Prompt:

Who in your life needs to be sung to?

What would it feel like to hold a sound space in your living room, your barbershop, or your classroom?

Can you imagine a neighborhood where sound is the medicine, not the noise?

What sound would you create if you knew your entire community was listening and would echo it back to you?

What is one way you can bring collective sound into your neighborhood, circle, or family this month?

Community Sound Healing Toolkit
For Black Healers, Organizers, and Spiritual Leaders

Core Principles
1. Sound is sacred.
2. Everyone has a voice.
3. The community is the healer.
4. No expertise required—only intention and presence.

1. Sound Circle Format (60-90 minutes)
Opening (10 min)
- Grounding breath: 3 deep breaths together
- Centering hum: Everyone hums low together.
- Opening affirmation (spoken together): "We are here. We are safe. We are sound."

Sound Flow (40–60 min)
Call & Response (5–10 min)
The facilitator begins with a phrase (sung, chanted, or spoken): "I am healing."
Group echoes: "I am healing."

Let this build into rhythm and improvisation.

Drumming/Rhythm Segment (15–20 min)
- Pass out drums, shakers, or use body percussion.
- Begin with heartbeat rhythm (Boom... Boom... Boom Boom... Boom)
- Let the group build its rhythm.
- Add foot stomps, hand claps, and voice.

The facilitator can guide with: "Let the ancestors move through your hands."

Vocal Expression & Moan Circle (10–15 min)

- Invite moaning, humming, and spontaneous singing
- Group sings or chants together, unscripted
- No right or wrong sound, just resonance

Encourage phrases like: "Let it out." "Sound what you feel." "No silence in this circle."

Stillness & Listening (5 min)

- Total silence
- Allow the breath to settle
- Invite tears, reflection, and presence

Closing (10 min)

- Each person speaks one word they feel (e.g., "Free," "Seen," "Whole")
- Pour libation or place a hand on the heart together
- Closing affirmation: "We carry the sound. We carry each other."

2. Basic Materials List

Type	Examples
Instruments:	Djembes, frame drums, shakers, tambourines, buckets, spoons, hands
Voice Tools:	Microphone (optional), megaphone, affirmation cards
Atmosphere:	Pillows, floor mats, candles, cloth, altar space
Audio Tools:	Bluetooth speaker (for sound bowls or tones), phone with playlist of frequencies
Visual Focus:	Ancestor photo, Kente cloth, symbolic item (feather, bowl of water)

3. Suggested Role

Role	Description
Facilitator	Holds rhythm, sets intention, guides energy flow
Timekeeper	Keeps the session on schedule without breaking the vibe
Sound Keeper	Passes out and gathers instruments, maintains instrument table
Elder/ Ancestor Witness	Opens/Closes with prayer, quote, or word from the ancestors
Vibe Keeper	Notices when someone needs support and offers quiet grounding

4. Formats and Occasions

- Healing After Violence or Loss (grief release circle)
- Celebration of Life / Ancestor Honoring
- Youth Empowerment Sound Circles
- Reentry/Reintegration Sound Sessions
- Family Healing Retreats
- Protest/Justice Movement Sound Prep

5. Sound Circle Guidelines

- No one is forced to speak or sound.
- Honor the silence when it comes.
- All emotions are welcome.
- Every sound is sacred, off-key, off-rhythm, and all.
- What happens in the circle stays in the circle.

CHAPTER NINE

RETURNING HOME TO SOUND AS AN ANCESTRAL PATHWAY

Legacies are not only written in words or recorded in history books; they are carried in the songs we remember, as well as the rhythms our hands still know, and the vibrations that live in our bones. For Black people, sound has always been both a bridge to the past and a healing gift for the future. It is how we have remembered who we are, even when the world tried to make us forget. It is how we have passed on not just culture, but survival itself.

The sound healing traditions we carry are ancient. They are older than any written scripture and older than any empire. They were born from the frequencies in the temples of the Nile Valley, the drum rituals of West Africa, and the ululations of celebration in villages across the African continent. They traveled across the Atlantic in the holds of ships, hidden in the hums and moans of those who refused to let their spirit die. They took root in the hush harbors of the enslaved, in the shouts and claps of praise houses, in the ring shouts of the Gullah traditions from the Georgia Sea Islands, and the blues songs of the Delta.

Every generation has faced the question of whether these traditions will survive, and every generation has answered by making them their own sound. Our grandparents sang hymns over washboards. Our parents kept the rhythm alive in church choirs and on front porches. Today, we see it in gospel hip-hop fusions, in community drum circles, in healing workshops, in the call-and-response of a protest crowd. The form changes, but the heartbeat stays the same.

Preserving this legacy is not only about archiving it; it is about living it. A song on a shelf is silent; a drum in storage makes no sound. The traditions survive because we use them. We teach children not in the abstract, but in the kitchen while cooking, in the pew while waiting for service to start on the street corner, and while laughing with friends. We pass them on by embodying them, by making them a part of daily life rather than a rare performance.

Passing on the legacy also means making it accessible. The sounds of healing must belong to everyone in the community, not just trained musicians or spiritual leaders. Every voice is worthy, every hand can keep a beat. The beauty of African sound traditions lies in the fact that they were never meant to be exclusive—they were intended to be participatory. The most important gift we can give to the next generation is not the perfection of the sound, but the permission to create it.

In a world that often tells young Black people to quiet themselves, to tone down their voices, or to conform to standards that deny their cultural identity, teaching them the healing power of their own sound is a radical act. It tells them that their voice is medicine, their rhythm is history, and their song is a birthright. It tells them that the vibrations of their ancestors still move through them, waiting to be expressed.

Maintaining and passing on this legacy is also about more than tradition; it is about survival in a changing world. Technology can connect us, but it can also isolate us. Digital spaces can carry our music around the world, but they cannot replace the feeling of voices and drums vibrating in the same room. We must be intentional about creating spaces where we gather in person, where we breathe the same air, where our sounds mix and mingle in real time. This is where the most profound healing happens.

And perhaps most importantly, we must remember that sound healing is not just for moments of crisis; it is for every season of life. We use it to celebrate births, honor deaths, mark transitions, strengthen movements, and comfort one another in grief. By weaving sound into our daily rituals, such as morning prayers, family dinners, and community meetings, we ensure that the legacy is not something we dust off for special occasions, but something we live with every day.

When we pass on the songs, rhythms, and chants of our people, we are doing more than preserving culture; we are preparing the next generation to face the world with tools of resilience, joy, and connection. We are giving them a map back to themselves, no matter how far they travel.

The healing power of sound is not a thing of the past; it is a living, breathing force. It is the hum of your grandmother while she works, the chant of the crowd calling for justice, the drumbeat that calls you to dance when you thought you were too tired. It is in you right now, as you read these words. And the legacy will continue, as long as we keep making the sound. This chapter is not about a new technique. It is an invitation to reclaim sound as a pathway to spiritual, cultural, and ancestral homecoming.

Sound Is a Living Archive

Within our sound, our voice, our music, our rhythms, lives are encoded in memory. These are not just emotional memories, but ancestral, cellular, and spiritual ones. When we chant a name, strike a drum, or sing a spiritual, we are not just making noise; we are activating ancestral archives. We are remembering something that colonialism, forced migration, and silence tried to erase. And yet, it remains. Beneath the surface. Waiting to be sounded back into form.

Our Bodies Remember

The Black body is not simply a site of trauma. It is a temple of remembering. The breath, the pulse, and the vibration in our chest when we sing are all ancestral technologies. You may not speak Twi, Yoruba, Kikongo, or Kiswahili. You may not know the names of your great-grandmothers. But when you moan in prayer, stomp your feet in rhythm, sing in church with tears in your throat, and chant "asé" or "hallelujah," you are speaking in the tongue of those who came before. Even in loss, the body remembers.

The Sound Within Our Bones

Long before we spoke a word, we were vibration. In the womb, we responded to rhythm. Our heartbeat is entrained to our mother's. Our cells moved to the music of life. That rhythm continues within us now.

Black people carry the sounds of survival and spirit in our bones. The echo of the djembe, the whisper of gospel moans, and the breath of the ancestors calling our names. To return to sound is to return to ourselves, not as broken people seeking healing, but as divine beings remembering our wholeness.

Sound as a Bridge Across Time

When we hum the old songs, chant the ancient names, or beat the sacred rhythm, we are not performing, we are communing. Sound collapses time. It links the past, present, and future in one vibration.

A spiritual song sung today still carries the sound frequency of the field. A drumbeat in Oakland, California, USA, still echoes in Accra, Ghana. A whisper in prayer still resonates with the voices of those who prayed for us here. Through sound, the veil is thinned. The ancestors listen. And if we listen closely, they respond.

Sacred Remembering Practices

To make sound sacred again is to create space in your life for ritualized vibration. It can be small. It can be simple. But it must be intentional. Here are a few ancestral homecoming practices:

Daily Morning Hum
Begin each day with 2 minutes of humming while your hand rests on your heart. "I return. I remember. I rise."

Ancestor Drumming
Each month, beat the drum for those who came before you. Call their names aloud. Let your rhythm be gratitude.

Speak Their Names
Create a sound altar. Light a candle. Say their names. Sing something they loved. Let their memory rise in your voice.

Full Moon Toning
On full moons, chant "AH" under the open sky. Let your voice join the frequency of the Earth and cosmos.

Why We Need a Sonic Return

We live in an era of overstimulation and profound fragmentation. Our people are facing generational grief, identity confusion, spiritual exhaustion, and disconnection from the land, language, and lineage.

We need to transition from treatment to ritual to heal ourselves. We need to reintroduce sound as a spiritual practice in our healing journey.

We must continue to research our past if we are to advance. Knowing that "it is not taboo to fetch what is at risk of being left behind," the Akan Sankofa adage emphasizes the value of drawing lessons from the past to inform and forge a bright future. The book Ancient Future: The Teachings and Prophetic Wisdom of the Seven Hermetic Laws of Ancient Egypt by Wayne B. Chandler comes to mind when I think about this. Timeless order and knowledge are comprised of these seven Tehuti axioms: Mentalism, Correspondence, Vibration, Polarity, Gender, Rhythm, and Causation. However, simply being aware of them without taking appropriate action is useless.

Sound healing is a practice, not a cure. The growth of the mind alone cannot bring about transformation. To achieve a true metamorphosis and unification of our body, mind, and spirit, we must learn breathing techniques to enhance our internal and physical energy, practice meditation to calm and expand our mental faculties, and utilize specific movement skills to convey energy and strength. Let's return home and use sound as an ancestral pathway to heal.

Practices for the Sonic Path of Return

Here are five core practices for returning to your ancestral center using sound:

1. Ancestral Name Calling

Create space weekly or monthly to say the names of your elders and ancestors out loud. If you do not know them, speak generational roles: "Mother of my mother. Father of my father. The midwives who sang over me. The warriors who prayed for me here." Speak each name like a tone. Let it become music.

2. Elemental Sound Alignment

Pair sound with the four classical elements that African traditions recognize:

Element	Sound	Practice
Earth	Deep hum	Sit on the ground and hum while placing hands on thighs
Water	Flowing chant	Chant "Shu" or "Shoo" while rocking or swaying
Fire	Breath & rhythm	Clap or drum with fast, intentional breath
Air	Whispering prayer	Speak softly into your hands or the wind

3. Moon & Seasonal Sound Rituals

On the full moon or solstice, gather in silence, light candles, and chant: "I return to the rhythm.
I return to the root. I return to the ones who carried me." Let everyone in the circle add a sound, name, or beat. This becomes an ancestral offering.

4. Sacred Sound Altars

Build an altar with:
- A bowl of water
- Bells or tuning forks
- A piece of African cloth
- A small drum or shaker
- A photo of an ancestor

Each morning, strike the bell, say a name, and speak an intention: "May this day carry their wisdom through my voice."

5. Ancestor Music Playlist

Create a playlist that reflects your heritage. Include:

- Traditional African drumming
- Spirituals
- Gospel classics
- Jazz, soul, or blues from your family era

Play it weekly and let yourself feel, cry, sing, or move.

Sound as Liberation, Not Just Healing

For Black people, sound is a form of emancipation, as it provides a means to express unity and resistance, maintain their cultural identity, and develop emotional and spiritual resilience in the face of injustice. Black people have transformed everyday experiences into powerful movements for social and political change by expressing their experiences of injustice and longing for liberation through musical genres such as gospel, jazz, blues, and spirituals. This journey is about feeling better. It is about becoming free. When we sound intentionally, we reclaim spiritual agency, break generational silence, reprogram trauma with vibration, and awaken the ancestral DNA within. This is not performance. This is prophecy.

You have read the words. Felt the rhythm. Touched the memory. Now, the sound that will heal your lineage, your family, and your neighborhood is within you. It is waiting to be expressed, carried, and amplified. Do not wait for permission. Do not wait for perfection. Open your mouth. Strike your drum. Lift your voice. Return home. And bring others with you.

Sound and Epigenetic Memory

Modern science is now validating what African wisdom has always known: we inherit more than genetics, we inherit vibration. Sound can awaken epigenetic memory, unlocking frozen energy stored in the body from past generations. When you release your voice, you may also be releasing the silence of a grandmother and honoring a warrior who was never named. Or singing the joy that an ancestor was denied. In sound, you are not just healing yourself; you are also healing others. You are freeing the entire line.

The Journey Forward Is a Journey Back

Our healing must be cyclical, not linear. Western models often aim for a finish line: "I'm healed now." But ancestral healing says, "Keep returning. Keep sounding. Keep listening." You do not need to be a minister or therapist to walk this path. You are enough. Your sound is enough. Your heart knows what it came here to remember. This book has not asked you to master anything. It has asked you to reawaken. To re-tune. To re-sound your sacred truth.

Final Call:

- May you moan when the silence is too heavy.
- May you drum when the pulse needs revival.
- May you sing when grief needs movement.
- May you speak when others are afraid to.

Because your sound is the revolution.
Your sound is the return.

Final Reflection:

What is the one sound, one chant, one drumbeat, one whispered name, that always brings you home?

What sound will you leave for the next generation to remember you by?

What vibration do you want your life to carry?

SOUND HEALING FOR THE BLACK PROFESSIONAL ATHLETE

The roar of the crowd. The squeak of sneakers on the court. The crack of the bat. The thunder of feet pounding the track. For professional athletes, sound is part of the game. But behind the applause and highlight reels, there are other sounds, quieter, more personal that often go unheard: the breath held in moments of high pressure, the internal monologue before a critical play, the silence that follows defeat.

For Black professional athletes, the journey to the top is not only physical, but also mental, emotional, and spiritual. Their bodies are their livelihood, but their minds and spirits carry the weight of performance expectations, racial stereotypes, systemic inequalities, and the pressure of representing far more than themselves. The field or court is never just a field or court; it is a stage where every move is scrutinized, every word dissected, every gesture magnified.

Although I was not a professional athlete, I participated in track teams from elementary school through senior high school and throughout my four years of college, primarily as a triple jumper. I came to realize that it was not just about my physical performance, but also about how emotionally calm I remained, regardless of the outcome.

Sound healing and mindfulness offer a powerful counterbalance to this environment. It provides a space where the body can release the tension that accumulates from the demands of competition, where the mind can quiet the noise of external judgment, and where the spirit can reconnect to a sense of wholeness beyond wins and losses.

Control Emotions Using Sound Therapy

Sports psychologists employ a range of methods to help professional athletes manage their emotions, including sound therapy that utilizes music, ambient noise, or binaural beats to reduce stress and enhance performance. By stimulating the parasympathetic nervous system, these audio interventions can help lower blood pressure, slow the heart rate, and promote relaxation. To increase resilience and focus, athletes can also utilize self-talk, goal-setting, and positive imagery. They can even pinpoint sounds or songs that help them cope with stress, worry, and rage.

By stimulating the parasympathetic nervous system, which lowers blood pressure and slows the pulse rate, relaxing noises and music can help the body transition from a state of high alertness and stress to a more relaxed one. According to studies, athletes' stress, rage, and anxiety can be considerably reduced by sound meditation and other sound therapies. Sounds can help athletes focus and concentrate better during training and competition by establishing a calm baseline. Certain types of music and noises can enhance endurance, reduce feelings of exhaustion, and improve overall performance. Athletes can benefit from auditory stimulation during their recuperation by retraining the central nervous system to generate more calm, parasympathetic states.

Utilizing music to control unpleasant emotions like rage, anxiety, or listening to customized music playlists to focus. Using ambient sounds, such as wind chimes or ocean drums, to promote profound relaxation.

Listening to binaural beats, which are tones that can help reset the brain's reaction to stress and induce a peaceful, meditative state. They can relieve tension by using sound baths and engaging in meditation, which uses vocal tones and sound instruments to promote profound relaxation and introspection.

Discover which types of music or sounds help you focus and manage your emotions most effectively. To aid in your emotional and physical preparation, include soothing audio in your pre-performance routine. During your workouts, play music or engage in other forms of auditory stimulation to enhance your endurance and manage fatigue. To encourage calmness, play relaxing music before bed or during stressful times, such as the sounds of the ocean or a forest.

Breathing Techniques

A sound healing practice for professional athletes and others includes breathing techniques. Healing is a process of regaining well-being. It involves the body's natural ability to repair itself. Healing is not to be equated with being cured. It is a return to a sense of balance. The best practice I know that we should all adopt is intentional breathing techniques. Here are some of my favorites:

- After a stressful physical activity or event, Box Breathing, also known as Square Breathing, is a breathing technique that can help calm the body and mind. By focusing on a 4-4-4-4 sequence of inhale, hold, exhale, hold, this technique slows down breathing and diverts the mind.
- A popular breathing exercise in yoga, the Breath of Fire technique is characterized by its quick and rhythmic nature. It involves rapid, forceful exhalations that engage the diaphragm and abdominal muscles.

- Alternative Nostril Breathing: Use your thumb to shut your right nostril. Through your left nostril, take a slow breath. Exhale slowly from your right nostril after closing your left with your index finger. For multiple rounds, alternate your nostrils.

A key element of breath control is expanding the diaphragm when inhaling and shrinking the lower stomach muscle when exhaling. The exhale should be 3 to 5 times longer than the inhale. The deliberate, ongoing endeavor to improve the healing process is known as intentional healing. The method of healing is natural. Supporting the body's natural healing process with mindfulness is known as deliberate healing.

The Pressure of the Spotlight

Black athletes often carry a dual weight: the weight of their performance and the weight of representing their communities in spaces that have historically excluded them. This dual role can create chronic stress that takes a toll on the body and mind. Even with top-tier physical training and medical care, the nervous system can remain in a constant state of "fight or flight," leading to burnout, injury, or mental exhaustion.

Sound healing, whether through drumming, chanting, guided meditation, or harmonic resonance, works directly on the nervous system. Vibrations help shift the body out of survival mode and into a state of rest, repair, and regeneration. For athletes whose bodies are pushed to the edge daily, this recovery is not a luxury; it is a necessity.

The Healing of Identity

In professional sports, Black athletes are often reduced to their physical abilities. The humanity, complexity, and cultural identity behind the jersey can be overlooked. Sound healing offers a way to reclaim that identity. African drumming patterns, ancestral chants, or gospel harmonies can reconnect an athlete to their heritage, reminding them that their worth is rooted in who they are, not just in what they can do.

These sounds act as cultural anchors, grounding the athlete in a lineage of strength and resilience that extends beyond the game. They remind the athlete that they are part of a continuum that their story is connected to the stories of those who came before them and those who will follow.

Team Cohesion and Collective Rhythm

Sports teams thrive on chemistry. A group of individuals must learn to move as one unit, anticipate each other's actions, and communicate without words. Sound healing practices, particularly rhythmic exercises such as group drumming, can foster cohesion. When a team synchronizes its rhythms, it also synchronizes its focus and energy. The sense of unity that emerges on the drum can translate directly to better performance on the field or court.

For Black athletes on diverse teams, these practices can also serve as cultural bridges, introducing teammates to African diasporic sound traditions while creating a shared experience that strengthens bonds.

Mental Resilience and Focus

The mental demands of professional sports are enormous. Distractions, hostile crowds, and high-stakes moments require focus under pressure. Sound-based meditation, such as tonal humming, overtone chanting, or binaural beats, can help athletes train their attention, regulate their breathing, and enter a "flow state" more easily.

For Black athletes who also contend with racialized heckling or biased officiating, these techniques can serve as emotional armor, helping them stay centered in their energy, unaffected by external hostility.

Post-Career Healing

Retirement from professional sports can be a sudden and profound shock to the system. Without the structure of daily training and the adrenaline of competition, many athletes experience a loss of identity, purpose, or community. Sound healing can help ease this transition by providing new rhythms and rituals that sustain mental, emotional, and spiritual well-being beyond the game.

It can also offer a way to give back; retired athletes can bring sound healing into youth programs, schools, and community centers, passing on both athletic wisdom and cultural healing practices to the next generation.

A Holistic Performance Edge

Ultimately, sound healing is not separate from athletic performance, it is an integral part of it. By restoring balance to the nervous system, reconnecting athletes to their heritage, building team cohesion, and sharpening mental focus, sound healing becomes a holistic performance tool. For Black professional athletes, it is also an act of self-preservation in an industry that can easily consume them.

To enhance health and well-being, Qigong is another traditional practice that incorporates breathing exercises, meditation, gentle movements, and sounds, making it a valuable addition for professional athletes. It is predicated on the idea that vital energy, or "qi," circulates throughout the body. I incorporate the Six Sounds of Qigong in my sound therapy sessions. This practice, rooted in traditional Chinese medicine, utilizes specific vocal sounds in conjunction with postures to release negative emotions and detoxify the body's energetic systems.

Organ	Element	Sound	Positive Emotion	Negative Emotion
Lungs	Air	Zzzzz	Courage	Sadness
Kidneys	Water	Shooo	Creativity	Fear
Liver	Wood/ Earth	Shhhh	Kindness	Anger
Heart	Fire	Haaaa	Joy	Impatience
Spleen	Earth	Chooo	Balance	Worry
Triple Warmer	Ether	X	X	X

Being mindful, with the practice of breathing and meditation, involves focusing on the present moment without passing judgment. It aims to cultivate awareness of one's thoughts, emotions, physical experiences, and external influences. Enhances focus and concentration while lowering tension and anxiety. Improves the control of emotions. Enhances overall health and well-being, promoting self-acceptance and self-compassion.

The sound of the crowd may fade. The stats may be forgotten. But the inner sound, the steady rhythm of the heart, the ancestral beat in the bones, remains. And that sound, when nurtured, becomes the foundation not just for winning games, but for living whole, healthy, and free.

GUIDED PRACTICE
Sound Healing for Athletes

Purpose: To restore balance, release physical and mental tension, and reconnect to personal and ancestral strength.

Time Needed: 15–20 minutes

Materials:
- A comfortable, quiet space (locker room, hotel room, gym studio, or even outdoors)
- A small drum (djembe, frame drum) or access to a low-vibration sound (bass tone, subwoofer, or drum loop)
- Optional: eye mask, yoga mat, or towel to lie down on

Step 1: Grounding the Body (2 minutes)
1. Stand or sit comfortably with feet flat on the ground.
2. Close your eyes and take three deep breaths, inhale through the nose, exhale through the mouth.
3. As you breathe, imagine roots growing from your feet deep into the earth. With each exhale, release the stress of travel, media attention, and competition into the ground.

Step 2: The Heartbeat Connection (3 minutes)
1. Begin playing or listening to a slow, steady drumbeat at about 60 beats per minute, matching a resting heart rate.
2. Place one hand on your chest and feel your heartbeat syncing with the rhythm.
3. With each beat, silently affirm:

I am steady. I am strong. I am present.

Step 3: Breath and Tone Release (4 minutes)

1. Inhale deeply through the nose, filling your lungs.
2. On the exhale, make a deep humming sound ("mmm") and feel the vibration in your chest, jaw, and skull.
3. Repeat for several breaths, allowing the sound to increase in volume slightly each time.
4. Imagine the hum loosening tight muscles, easing joint tension, and clearing mental clutter.

Step 4: Power Chant (3 minutes)

1. Choose a word or short phrase that fuels your confidence, examples: *Rise, Power, Unstoppable, Asé*.
2. On each exhale, chant the word in a steady rhythm with the drumbeat.
3. Feel the sound vibrating in your core and radiating outward into your limbs.
4. With each repetition, stand taller and embody the meaning of the word.

Step 5: Ancestral Rhythm Activation (4 minutes)

1. Shift to a faster drum rhythm (90–110 beats per minute) to energize the body.
2. If you have a drum, play along; if not, clap, tap your thighs, or stomp lightly.
3. With each beat, visualize ancestors standing behind you, athletes, warriors, and elders who paved the way for you.
4. Feel their strength moving into your muscles, their courage filling your lungs, their focus sharpening your mind.

Step 6: Closing Integration (3–4 minutes)

1. Return to a slow heartbeat rhythm.
2. Place one hand on your heart, one on your belly.
3. Whisper to yourself: *I carry my strength within. My sound protects me. My rhythm is my power.*
4. Sit or stand in silence for one minute, letting the vibrations settle into your body.

Post-Practice Tip:

- If this is done before a game, carry a small "sound token" with you (like a crystal stone, a tuning fork, or a recording of a short chant) to recall the energy during competition.
- If after a game, extend the slow, grounding section for deeper recovery.

FOR THE BLACK PROFESSIONAL

Introduction

In the fast-paced, high-stress environments where many Black professionals live and work, mindfulness is more than a wellness trend; it is an act of healing, self-preservation, and empowerment. The practice of mindfulness involves focusing on the present moment with intention and without judgment, noticing your thoughts, feelings, and environment without becoming entangled in them. It is a valuable ability to incorporate into everyday tasks, helping people to focus better, manage stress, promote wellbeing, and become more self-aware. Rooted in both African ancestral traditions and contemporary practices, mindfulness can restore balance, reduce stress, and deepen connection to purpose.

1. Centering Breath Practice (Ancestral Breathwork)

Purpose: Release tension, ground in the present, and connect with ancestral strength.

Practice:
- Sit upright with both feet on the ground.
- Close your eyes and place your right hand on your heart, and the left hand on your belly.

- Inhale slowly through the nose, imagining you are drawing breath from the Earth itself.
- Exhale through the mouth with a gentle sigh, releasing stress.
- Repeat for 7–10 breaths, silently affirming: *I breathe with the wisdom of my ancestors.*

2. Morning Grounding Ritual

Purpose: Begin each workday with clarity and intention.

Practice:

- Before checking emails or rushing, stand near a window or step outside.
- Place your palms together at your chest.
- Speak aloud an intention for the day (e.g., *"Today, I walk in confidence and peace"*).
- Take three deep breaths and step into your day with focus.

3. Sound Vibration Reset (Midday Practice)

Purpose: Use sound to realign the nervous system and reset the workday.

Practice:

- Find a quiet space (even a restroom or parked car).
- Inhale deeply, then hum a steady tone (such as *"mmm"* or *"aum"*) for the length of your exhale.
- Feel the vibration in your chest, throat, and head.
- Repeat 3–5 times.
- Variation: Play a calming African drum rhythm or an ancestral chant recording to realign focus.

4. Stress Release Through Movement

Purpose: Release built-up physical stress from microaggressions, meetings, or workload.

Practice:

- Stand and gently roll your shoulders backward five times, then forward five times.
- Gently shake out your arms and legs, releasing any tension.
- Place both feet firmly on the ground and sway side to side as if in rhythm with a drum.
- Close with three deep breaths, arms raised overhead.

5. Evening Gratitude Reflection

Purpose: Close the workday with peace, self-compassion, and grounding.

Practice:

- In a journal or voice note, name three things you are grateful for in the day.
- Acknowledge one challenge you faced and what it taught you.
- Take a final deep breath and say: *I give thanks to the ancestors and elders.*

6. Community Practice (Weekly Ritual)

Purpose: Heal together by connecting with other Black professionals.

Practice:

- Gather virtually or in person once a week.
- Open with a grounding breath and/or drumming track.
- Share one word that describes your week.
- Close with a collective affirmation: *Harambee* (*let's all pull together as one*).

Closing Affirmation

I am present, I am centered, I carry the strength of generations. Each breath, each sound, each healing practice restores me.

THE SOUND CONTINUES

Sound is the first thing we hear when we enter this world, the steady heartbeat of our mother, pulsing in the darkness before birth. And it will be among the last things we hear before we leave, voices gathered around, speaking our name, singing us home. Between those two moments, sound is our constant companion. It marks our milestones, carries our stories, and reminds us of who we are.

For the Black community, sound has been more than an expression; it has been a means of survival. It has been our coded message, our battle cry, our lullaby, our medicine. It has been the drum that called us to gather, the hymn that steadied our grief, the chant that shook the walls of oppression, the voice that refused to be silenced.

This book has been a journey through those sounds, ancient African healing practices, the science of rhythm in the Black body, the role of drums in liberation, the sacred soundscape of the Black church, the chants and beats of protest, the medicine of the human voice, and the way our collective sound can restore an entire community. We have examined the legacy that brought us here and the responsibility we bear in passing it on.

But these pages are not the end of the story. They are an invitation. An invitation to open your mouth and let your voice rise. An invitation to put your hands on a drum and feel the ancestors moving through your fingertips. An invitation to hum, to clap, to chant, to shout, to let the vibration in your body be heard and felt by others.

We do not heal in silence. We heal in sound. We heal when we join our voices with others, when we let rhythm align our hearts, when we create spaces where every sound, every moan, every cry, every laugh, is welcome.

The healing power of sound is not locked in history. It is here, now, in the beat of your own heart, in the breath you are taking at this moment. Every time you make a sound with intention, whether in a sanctuary, a protest, a classroom, or a circle of friends, you are continuing the work of those who came before you. You are keeping the ancestors alive.

One day, future generations will talk about how we utilized sound to heal ourselves and transform our communities. They will hum our songs, clap our rhythms, and speak our words. They will know that they are part of a long, unbroken chain of sound-makers, healers, and freedom-seekers.

So let us leave them more than our struggles, let us leave them our music, our chants, our drums, our laughter, our joy. Let us leave them a world that still vibrates with the truth that we were here, that we loved each other enough to keep singing, and that our sound could not be silenced.

Let us take this moment and breathe together as one. The sound continues. And so do we.

GLOSSARY

This glossary includes spiritual, cultural, musical, and healing terms used throughout the book, defined with care for readers new to this work or those seeking to deepen their understanding.

Asé (A-shay): A Yoruba term meaning "so let it be," "power," or "the authority to command spiritual energy." Used to affirm truth, prayer, and intention.

Binaural Beats: An auditory phenomenon where your brain perceives a third, different-frequency sound when two tones of slightly different frequencies are presented separately to each ear, requiring headphones to experience.

Call-and-Response: A traditional musical structure where one voice or instrument "calls" and another answers. Found in African, African American, and Afro-Caribbean music, this structure supports communal sound-making and energetic exchange.

Chakra: In yogic traditions, energy centers in the body. In sound healing, specific tones and frequencies are associated with these centers to aid in balance and alignment.

Djembe: A goblet-shaped hand drum originating from West Africa, used in healing, celebration, and spiritual ritual.

Drum Circle: A collective rhythmic gathering where participants play drums or percussion instruments. Used for emotional release, community building, and energetic regulation.

Epigenetics: The study of how trauma, stress, or environmental factors can impact gene expression is often used to explain generational trauma in marginalized communities.

Frequency: The rate of vibration or oscillation. In sound healing, different frequencies have unique effects on the body and mind (e.g., 528 Hz is associated with love healing and DNA repair).

Griot (Gree ow): A West African oral historian, storyteller, and musician who preserves community memory and cultural knowledge through performance.

Humming: A gentle vocal vibration is often used in sound healing to stimulate the vagus nerve and calm the nervous system.

Liberation Sound: A term used in this book to describe sonic expressions rooted in freedom, protest, resistance, and soul healing for Black people.

Moan: A deep, wordless vocalization of emotion often used in spiritual practice, Black church worship, and healing rituals to express grief, relief, or ecstasy.

Parasympathetic Nervous System: A network of nerves that connects the brain and spinal cord to various organs and tissues throughout the body.

Resonance: The way sound vibrates through a person or space. In healing, it refers to how certain tones or sounds "resonate" with parts of the body or spirit.

Sonic Identity: An individual or collective's unique vibration, voice, rhythm, or musical style that reflects cultural and spiritual lineage.

Sound Bath: A meditative experience where participants are "bathed" in healing sound waves from singing bowls, gongs, tuning forks, or voice.

Spirituals: Sacred songs developed by enslaved Africans in the Americas, used as coded language, resistance tools, and emotional expression.

Toning: The practice of sustaining a vowel sound (e.g., "AHHH" or "OOO") to balance energy in the body and activate healing vibrations.

Ubuntu: A quality that includes the essential human virtues: compassion and humanity. "I am because we are."

Vagus Nerve: A major nerve connecting the brain to the body. It regulates emotional responses and can be activated through breath, humming, or sound.

CHAKRA CHART

Delta Hz (1 - 4 Hz): The slowest and highest amplitude brain waves. Most prominent during sleep. It can help access information in the unconscious mind.

Theta Hz (4 - 8 Hz): The second slowest brain waves. Occurs during meditation, prayer, or spiritual awareness. These waves are associated with creativity, intuition, and fantasizing.

Alpha Hz (8 - 14 Hz): These waves are detected during relaxed states, such as when you are awake but not actively thinking. These waves are associated with a decreased perception of pain and discomfort.

Beta Hz. (14 - 30 Hz): are the most common brain waves in adults and children, associated with active thinking, being busy, or being anxious.

Gamma Hz (30 - 100 Hz) are the fastest brain waves and are associated with focus and higher brain functions.

Chakra Chart

Chakra	Location	Color	Frequency (Hz)	Element	Healing Focus
Root	Base of spine	Red	396 Hz	Earth	Grounding, security, survival
Sacral	Lower abdomen	Orange	417 Hz	Water	Creativity, sexuality, flow
Solar Plexus	Upper abdomen	Yellow	528 Hz	Fire	Confidence, power, will
Heart	Center of chest	Green	639 Hz	Air	Love, compassion, connection
Throat	Throat	Blue	741 Hz	Ether	Expression, truth, communication
Third Eye	Forehead, between eyes	Indigo	852 Hz	Light	Intuition, insight, wisdom
Crown	Top of head	Violet/White	963 Hz	Spirit	Oneness, divine connection

REFERENCES

& RESOURCES

Academic & Scientific Sources

1. Benenzon, R. O. (2014). *Music Therapy: Theory and Manual.* Barcelona Publishers.
2. Campbell, D. (2001). *The Mozart Effect.* HarperCollins.
3. Cross, I. (2006). Music and communication in music psychology. *Psychology of Music, 34*(4), 431–456.
4. Koen, B. D., Barz, G., & Brummel-Smith, K. (Eds.). (2008). *The Oxford Handbook of Medical Ethnomusicology.* Oxford University Press.
5. Thompson, W. F., & Schlaug, G. (2015). The healing power of music. *Scientific American Mind, 26*(5), 32–41.

African & African Diaspora Cultural Resources

6. Anyidoho, K. (1992). *The Word Behind Bars and the Paradox of Exile.* NorthwesternUniversity Press.
7. Chandler, W. B. (1999). *Ancient Future.* Black Classic Press
8. Elliott, T. (2019). *Spirit, Rhythm, and Story: Community Building and Healing through Song.* Covenant Books, Inc.
9. Floyd, S. (1995). *The Power of Black Music.* Oxford University Press.

10. Fu-Kiau, K. K. (2001). *African Cosmology of the Bantu-Kongo.* Athelia Henrietta Press.

11. Nketia, J. H. K. (1974). *The Music of Africa.* W.W. Norton & Company.

12. Rabaka, R. (2015). *The Hip Hop Movement: From R&B and the Civil Rights Movement to Rap and the Hip Hop Generation.* Lexington Books. 13. Van Sertima, I. (1976). *They Came Before Columbus.* Random House.

Sound Healing & Practical Application

13. Arewa, C. S. (1998). *Opening to Spirit.* Afrikan World Books.

14. Goldman, J. (2017). *The 7 Secrets of Sound Healing.* Hay House.

15. Halpern, S. (1985). *Sound Health.* Harper & Row.

16. Horowitz, L. (2011). *The Book of 528: Prosperity Key of Love.* Tetrahedron Publishing

17. Khan, H. I. (1983). *The Music of Life: The Inner Nature and Effects of Sound.* Sulük Press.

18. Knight, W. A. (2013). *Vibrational Healing Through the Chakras.* Inner Traditions.

19. Mannes, E. (2011). *The Power of Music: Pioneering Discoveries in the New Science of Song. Walker and Company.*

20. McClellan, R. (1999). *The Healing Forces of Music.* Amity House.

21. Murphy, B. D. (2015). The A = 432 Hz frequency: DNA tuning and the bastardization of music. *Waking Times.*

22. Wigram, T., Pedersen, I. N., & Bonde, L. O. (2002). *A Comprehensive Guide to Music*

23. *Therapy: Theory, Clinical Practice, Research and Training.* Jessica Kingsley Publishers.

Suggested Multimedia & Online Resources

24. Smithsonian Folkways Recordings – https://folkways.si.edu

25. African Music Archive (University of Mainz) – https://www.blogs.uni-mainz.de/african-music-

26. Healing Sounds by Jonathan Goldman – https://www.healingsounds.com

27. Playing for Change Foundation – https://playingforchange.org

ALBUM DESCRIPTION

Enhance your journey into sound healing. The companion album, *Soul Healing Jazz*, offers a restorative musical experience to accompany the book's teachings.

Album Description

Doc T Elliott—pianist, composer, and sound healer—crafted this digital album to realign the soul, soothe the spirit, and awaken ancestral memory.

Rooted in the rich legacy of Black musical traditions, this album blends the improvisational heart of jazz with the intentional vibration of healing frequencies. Each track is a journey—infused with spirit, layered with soul, and guided by a profound understanding of music as a transformative tool.

From meditative piano passages and ancestral drum rhythms to soaring horn lines and calming ambient textures, *Soul Healing Jazz* is both a personal invocation and a communal balm. Whether you need grounding, grieving, celebrating, or simply *being*, this album meets you where you are—and lifts you gently higher. "This isn't just jazz—it's healing encoded in harmony."

Please download this digital music album from various platforms, including iTunes, Apple Music, Spotify, and Pandora. This is my latest music source to be used in conjunction with this book for healing purposes.

Peace and blessings, Doc T Elliott

Books

Spirit, Rhythm, and Story: Community Building and Healing Through Song (2019)

Hip Hop Music: History and Culture, First Edition (2022), Second Edition (2025)

Music

Kissed by a Dove, Amanda Elliott (1999)

Cultural Consciousness, Black Song and Poetry (2002)

The New Jazz Swing (2005)

Jazz Nothin' But Soul (2013)

Music for the Soul: Relaxation & Meditation Songs (2015)

Soul Healing Jazz (2025)

www.ingramcontent.com/pod-product-compliance
Lightning Source LLC
Chambersburg PA
CBHW050448150626
46551CB00029B/1987